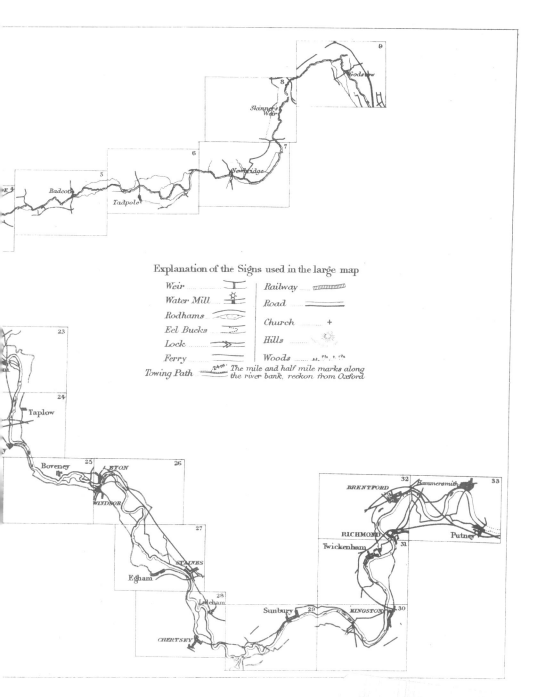

9

Godstow

8

Skinner's Weir

6

7

Newbridge

5

Radcot

Tadpole

E S

Explanation of the Signs used in the large map

Weir	⊥	Railway	▭
Water Mill	✳	Road	━
Rodhams	⌒		
Eel Bucks	⌐	Church	+
Lock	⇉	Hills	✳
Ferry	⟶	Woods	

Towing Path ·····24·M· The mile and half mile marks along the river bank, reckon from Oxford

23

24

Taplow

Boveney

25

ETON

26

WINDSOR

32

BRENTFORD

Hammersmith

33

RICHMOND

Putney

Twickenham

31

27

STAINES

Egham

28

Laleham

Sunbury

29

KINGSTON

30

CHERTSEY

THE THAMES
of
HENRY TAUNT

THE THAMES

of

HENRY TAUNT

Edited by

SUSAN
READ

ALAN SUTTON

First published in the United Kingdom in 1989
Alan Sutton Publishing Limited · Brunswick Road · Gloucester

First published in the United States of America in 1990
Alan Sutton Publishing Inc. · Wolfeboro Falls · NH 03896–0848

First published in this edition 1989

British Library Cataloguing in Publication Data

Taunt, Henry
    The Thames of Henry Taunt.
    England. Thames River. Description & travel
    I. Title   II. Read, Susan   III. Taunt, Henry. New map
    of the River Thames
    914.22'0481

    ISBN 0-86299-616-3

Library of Congress Cataloging in Publication Data
applied for

Typesetting and origination by
Alan Sutton Publishing Limited
Printed in Great Britain by WBC Print Ltd, Bristol

INTRODUCTION

To my many friends on the river, I heartily dedicate this little volume, which brings back to me many pleasing remembrances of kindness and welcome during forty years past and gone, and wishing every one of them many more happy outings on 'Tamise Streame'.

Thus Henry Taunt welcomed his readers in the preface of the sixth and last edition (1897) of *A New Map of the River Thames*.

Henry Taunt was born in 1842 in Penson's Gardens, St Ebbes, Oxford. His father a plumber by trade, was Oxfordshire born, while his mother had been brought up in the rural surroundings of the Berkshire Downs. His educational opportunities were rather limited but this fortunately was not to prove a handicap to an artistic and creative mind.

Taunt's decision not to follow his father's career allowed him the opportunity to experience various types of employment and ultimately to discover what was to offer him a creative and fulfilling future working life. In the mid-1850s he worked in the bookshop and auction rooms of Charles Richards in High Street, Oxford. Here he was to discover the delights of 'the book' in all its many guises. However, it was in 1856 that he took an important step which was to dramatically affect the pattern of his future. At this time he took employment with Edward Bracher who was a pioneer in the field of commercial photography in Oxford.

Initially he was employed to do general work at the photographic premises at 26 High Street, which was to provide a vital grounding in the understanding and appreciation of this rapidly developing art form. This was a most exciting period in the development of photography; the thrill generated by the discovery of the photographic process in 1839 was still present, but there was also a strong awareness that there was much more to be discovered and new ideas were continually being explored.

By the late 1850s Taunt was in charge of outdoor photographic work for Edward Bracher, for which he found a particular enthusiasm. It was this expertise in the field of topographical photography, developed over the following years, which was to prove invaluable in his later career.

When the well-known firm of Wheeler and Day took over the Bracher establishment, Taunt remained in the company's employ until in 1868 he was able to realize his ambition to set up his own business. By 1869 he had a collection of *Shilling Views of Oxford and the Neighbourhood* for sale, the quality of which was noticed and admired – 'We cannot but speak in terms of unqualified praise of the beauty of the views which were of unusual excellence' – *Oxford Times*. This was the beginning of an extensive collection of topographical views of Oxfordshire and the adjacent counties, with a particular emphasis on the River Thames. Success allowed Taunt to open a small shop at 33 Cornmarket Street, Oxford in 1869.

It was during the following years that his idea for *A New Map of the River Thames* was purposefully set in motion. Henry Taunt's interest in, and love of the River Thames had its origins in his childhood. Growing up in a Thames-side vicinity he had the opportunity to familiarize himself with many aspects of the river. A particular excursion in the winter of 1859 proved to be a memorable experience; 'We ran a few risks in our young days one way and another, but of them all the most venturesome was a solitary trip up the river to Cricklade and back at Christmas time in an outrigged dinghy.' Recording this some fifty years later he vividly portrayed the trip which turned out to be a gruelling, and nearly disastrous, undertaking due to the severity of the weather and the flood water conditions. Yet this experience was to enhance Taunt's great respect for this powerful river.

His deep personal feeling for the River Thames and the enthusiasm to share this with others can be clearly seen in a lecture entitled 'Trip down the Thames' which he gave shortly before the publication of the first edition of *A New Map of the River Thames*:

> The subject of my lecture this evening is one in which we are all interested and also one which the more we study the more numerous are the beauties we find in it. I ought perhaps to apologise for my boldness in attempting to place such an important subject before you but my excuse must be my love for it . . . .The Thames has been a very favourite study for some years and the leading idea I have tonight is, so to illustrate some few of its beauties as to lead some of you who have not looked so thoroughly into them, to step aside and throwing over perhaps the trip you had promised yourself in the ensuing summer deciding to have a trip up or down the Thames.

A guide, most suitably in book form, was a natural sequel to this encouraging suggestion, for Henry Taunt was well aware that he was not talking to the select few who had an interest in the Thames.

The idea of 'tourists' making excursions on the Thames appears to have become established from the beginning of the nineteenth century. Angling on the river dates back over a number of centuries and in 1838 the Thames Angling Preservation Society had been founded. During the eighteenth century various books and maps had been produced specifically on the Thames including *An History of the River Thames* by J. & J. Boydell, and *Picturesque Views of the River Thames* by Samuel Ireland, all reflecting an increasing interest in the subject. By the middle of the nineteenth century a number of volumes had been published concentrating on both the natural and the general history of the river and its adjacent towns and villages. Taunt himself mentions one published in the 1850s by Mr and Mrs S.C. Hall – *The Book of the Thames from its Rise to its Fall*. He felt that this had played its part in stimulating interest in the Thames, written in a charming style and beautifully illustrated with many engravings.

Taunt was obviously appreciative of such books as that by Mr and Mrs Hall, but he also saw the potential for a more practical, though equally attractive publication for the river user. Combining his knowledge of the river and his commercial instinct, he made a careful assessment of all the requisites of 'The Tourist, the Oarsman and the Angler'. Henry Taunt was a pioneer in the field of this type of companion guide to the River Thames, which would be taken up by other authors later in the century, in particular those produced by the well-known boat-hiring firm Salters of Oxford.

His approach to his guide was to base it on a series of thirty-three scale maps and this was particularly important. These were made from 'an entirely new survey taken during the summer of 1871'. In the preface to the first edition of *A New Map of the River Thames* he explained:

Originally I proposed to bring out a map of the river from its source at Trewsbury Mead to Putney, upon a scale of one inch to a mile: and in the intervals of photographing surveyed the greater part of the distance; but, finding that, where islands lay in the stream, or the way was barred by locks and weirs, it would be impossible on so small a scale to give accurate detail, only that portion of the river below Oxford has been brought out: but on a scale of two inches to the mile.

By the third edition published in 1879, based on a new survey in 1878, he was able to extend this as he had originally planned from 'Thames Head to London', though continuing to maintain throughout all editions the scale of two inches to the mile.

To accompany the maps Taunt provided timetables and details of distances between locks, ferries and bridges, the latter 'carefully chained along the Towing-path bank of the river'. Historical information and scenic guidance is given along the length of the river, though not without a passing criticism in order to assist the traveller on where and where not to linger.

To encourage the excursionist to 'camp-out' an additional chapter extolling the unforgettable pleasures of this experience, particularly if camping in one's boat rather than on land, is included. Among the original advertisements included in the book is one by John Salter of Oxford with detailed costs offering 'a pair-oared pleasure skiff fitted out with tent cover and mattress £3 15s. 0d.' for an excursion down the river from Oxford to Teddington which included cartage of the boat back to Oxford. For those wishing for greater comfort during their travels and for other river users such as anglers, Taunt provided a guide to suitable hotels and inns along the way. The advertisements for many of these establishments which appear in the book proffer their wares from luxury to homely comfort – The New Thames Hotel, Maidenhead 'specially for Families, Gentlemen and Boating Parties, Elegant Coffee Rooms and Private Sitting Rooms facing the River', and the King's Arms Hotel, Oxford 'For Families and Gentlemen. Old-fashioned, economical, comfortable and clean'. Intriguing and unforgettable names catch the eye, including the Beetle and Wedge at Moulsford Ferry, the Miller of Mansfield at Goring, the Flower Pot at Henley and the famous French Horn at Sonning.

Although Taunt was noticeably concerned with the needs of the tourist, he was also strongly aware of the tremendous scope of the River Thames for the angler. The abundance and variety of fish in the river in the nineteenth century is clearly shown and suitable, well-established fishermen are indicated for each stretch of water for the angler to contact when in need of assistance.

Bathing is another popular pursuit which Henry Taunt covered, an interest stemming back to his boyhood, for rivers were one of the major sources of this pleasure. However, he was extremely conscious of the hazards involved, and although he mentions many bathing-spots on the river, he also includes a strong cautionary comment: 'most of the weir pools on the Thames are capital places for a bathe to the strong swimmer, but timid ones ought in every case take the necessary precautions against danger, by bathing only in company and knowing the run of the place'.

During the 1880s tourism on the Thames accelerated and flourished. Opportunities to enjoy the pleasures of the river were extended to a larger proportion of the populace. The railway companies encouraged those from the towns to take advantage of their services to enjoy the countryside and particularly the River Thames. Licencing of pleasure boats of various types from skiffs to steam launches was formally established under the Thames Conservancy during the 1880s, for their numbers were continually increasing on the river. In such a climate Taunt's *A New Map of the River Thames* proved a highly popular venture, as the numerous editions clearly indicate. The sixth and last edition in 1897 commemorated its year of production as that of 'The Diamond Jubilee of Her Majesty'. Taunt was particularly concerned that, as with the previous editions, this volume had been most carefully brought up to date, including the maps. He also made some noticeable alterations in the photographs used in the previous edition.

Henry Taunt saw the inclusion of nearly a hundred of his photographs as companions to his maps as a most important element in his book. His continual emphasis on photographs shows both his own appreciation of these and a desire to share his pleasure with as many others as possible. By now his skill was well acclaimed and, in 1871, he became the official photographer to the Oxford Architectural and Historical Society. Being commercially minded he continued to develop and expand his business, but one is constantly aware of the genuine pleasure that he took in his work, and in particular in his photographs. From the early days of *The Shilling Series* he extended his repertoire to include richly bound albums. Morocco, Persian and Russian bindings which contained up to one hundred and eighty views of the Thames in each.

One cannot underestimate the skill and expertise, but also the perseverance and determination of the early outdoor photographer. Prior to the discovery of the gelatin emulsion process and its commercial availability in the 1870s, photography required carrying a portable darkroom out in the field as the earlier wet collodian method required sensitizing the plates immediately before exposure and developing directly afterwards. Even after this date, when the glass plates could be prepared in advance, the general weight and cumbersome nature of early photographic equipment should not be forgotten, however beautiful a mahogany and brass camera might appear. Henry Taunt managed to convey himself and his equipment, with the help of an assistant, by tricycle or in later years on the river he set up a small travelling houseboat – a well deserved note of luxury. His negatives from throughout his career number in the region of 53,000 and a considerable quantity were devoted to the subject of 'The Thames and its towns from Thames Head to the Nore.'

Throughout the latter part of the nineteenth century and early into this century Henry Taunt's business continued to flourish and expand. In 1874 he moved to 9 and 10 Broad Street, a large shop which offered more potential than the premises in Cornmarket Street. While he was working on various small catalogues and guides he became interested in the possibility of not only publishing but printing his own works. Despite a temporary setback caused by severe financial difficulties, he established a photographic and printing works at a large house appropriately renamed 'Rivera', on the Cowley Road, Oxford. Publications produced from here included later editions of his *A New*

THE THAMES OF HENRY TAUNT

Map of the River Thames, Tamesis, the River Thames illustrated with Camera and Pen and a new series of Historical Handbooks, each concentrating on a stretch of the Thames. He also ventured into the area of postcards which were to become universally popular. It was World War I which took its toll on the business, affecting sales and disrupting staff. Taunt himself was no longer a young man and after the war it proved impossible for the firm to regain its previous position. He died in 1922.

Henry Taunt's enthusiasm for life, his commercial acumen as well as his social awareness are some of the qualities for which he is remembered. He made his name in Oxford and beyond during his lifetime. He was an historian, a naturalist and a cartographer and was made a Fellow of the Royal Geographical Society in 1893. It is thought that his work for *A New Map of the River Thames* may have been responsible for this award. His lectures were not confined to the subject of the River Thames, for he is well-remembered for a variety of magic lantern shows, particularly to children in Oxford Town Hall. A man of music, he was an organist and amongst other compositions wrote a revised version of the National Anthem. In a somewhat different vein, he took an active interest in local politics in the city of Oxford. His photographs live with us as a continual reminder of his artistic skill and his overwhelming appreciation of each subject or view taken. 'Among them are some which for softness and clearness of detail as well as effective reproduction of light and shade rival in beauty the work of the most skillful draughtsman', *The Field* 1871.

Though written by Henry Taunt in 1900 in the preface to his series of 'Historical Handbooks' the following words convey the feelings of the author and apply equally well to his *A New Map of the River Thames*. 'A pleasant journey is made doubly enjoyable when an agreeable companion who is thoroughly acquainted with the objects of interest and their story is with us, scenes which are beautiful seem even more charming, in the society of a sympathetic friend, and more than half the pleasure of life is found in sharing our happiness with those around us.'

This edition of *A New Map of the River Thames* is taken from the fifth edition published 1886/1887 with some shortening of the original text and number of advertisements. However, additional material includes a selection of photographs of the Thames taken by Henry Taunt through his working life, and explanatory notes to accompany his commentary.

The Upper Thames, from Thames Head to Oxford

'From his oozy bed Old Father Thames advanced his rev'rend head.'
ALEXANDER POPE

THAMES HEAD to Cricklade *11 miles 6 furlongs 2 yards*

The greater part of the bank of the stream can be traversed after the grass is mown in the meadows.

The Thames rises in a very pretty valley-mead, bordered with trees, its source being in the parish of Coates, and county of Gloucester, amongst the Western Cotswolds, but by no means the highest part of that hill-group. The first of the four principal springs which forms its stream issues from a small well, from which, in 1885, was cleared the stones that for a number of years had entirely filled it up. The well is prettily shaded by some thorny bushes growing under and round a fair-sized tree close to the rising bank of the canal. In olden times, before the construction of the navigation, this spring would often be flowing; but owing to the action of the Thames Head Pump, which drains the water out of the springs, it only runs at rare intervals, and these only when the pump is still. The springs of the valley appear to have diminished in volume and force, and the water of this upper spring, which at one time was utilized for cattle in a cistern often overflowing, now seems to have sunk far below the surface; and it is not until we reach the fourth spring, more than a mile below, that in summer any signs of water may be seen beyond the rank grass that always springs up in flooded meadows, and the rough sedgy plants that grow in the dry river-bed before reaching that place. But in times of wet winter weather the scene is changed. The winter flow of the Churn at Cirencester with the land springs, and the drainage from the higher fields, supply the waste of the canal; the pump is no longer required;

1

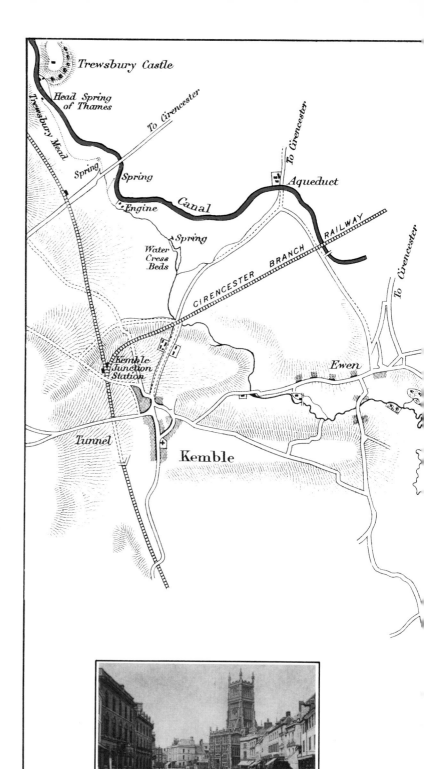

Trewsbury Castle

Head Spring
of Thames

Trewsbury Mead

To Cirencester

Spring

Spring

Canal

To Cirencester

Aqueduct

Engine

Spring

Water
Cress
Beds

CIRENCESTER BRANCH RAILWAY

To Cirencester

Kemble
Junction
Station

Ewen

Tunnel

Kemble

CIRENCESTER

THAMES HEAD

VIEW FROM THAMES HEAD BRIDGE

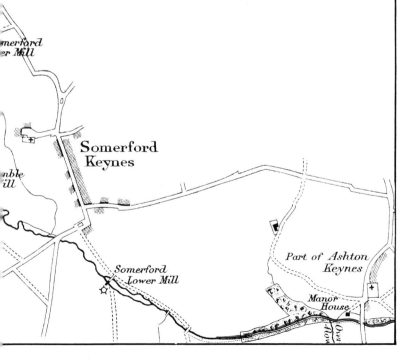

then the head springs burst forth, and the valley is flooded, so that the little arch beneath the road is altogether insufficient to carry away the accumulated waters. These winter floods thus pent back cover the river meadows, adding to their fertility, and the little channel in whose dry bed we may walk through the long days of summer, becomes the centre of a rushing stream.

We have already mentioned that the Thames is formed at its head by four principal springs: the first above described; the second, half a mile below, in the summer forming a kind of hollow basin in the ground, close to the Roman road from Cirencester to Tetbury; the third springs from the side of a hill just below the road; and the fourth, some distance lower down, just above the watercress bed, is the most powerful of them all, and rarely fails. These springs are helped by many others all over the valley, and we notice a curious phenomenon, which proves their fulness and force. The grass-covered ground in places looks baggy, and small hillocks are formed at intervals, which resemble a sponge when filled with water. Standing on one we force a stick for some distance through its covering of turf, and on withdrawing it, a fountain of water suddenly spurts out to the height of perhaps two feet, and continues gushing up for some time, until the hillock on which we stand has sunk down to the level of the mead around. The old Roman Fosse Way from Cirencester to Bath running straight over hill and dale, crosses the Thames and arches it over for the first time, the road here forming the boundary between the counties of Gloucester and Wiltshire. Our stream, having risen in the former county, soon makes its way into the latter, where it continues to wander and flow until near Lechlade, and then it becomes the boundary between Gloucestershire and Berkshire.

There has been much discussion as to which should be considered the head waters of the Thames, whether this or the Churn, rising at Seven Springs, near Cheltenham; also on the question whether the river should be called Thames or Isis on its upper part, before joining the Thame near Dorchester. Without entering deeply into this matter, we would call attention to the fact that these Cotswold springs rising near Coates have been called Thames Head, and the stream formed by them the Thames, from time immemorial, whereas the other head is called the Seven Springs, and the stream issuing from it the Churn. Moreover, the stream from Thames Head is considerably larger than the Churn where their waters unite at Cricklade; and this is even more apparent in times of flood, when the engine at Thames Head is still. As to the name, old records at Oxford and far above call it Thames, and surely a river rising at 'Thames Head' ought not to change its name into the classic Isis, and afterwards re-assume its patronymic of Thames. The Thame at the junction is a rivulet compared with the Thames: indeed, it is so small that the mouth is often overlooked by oarsmen passing up the parent stream, even though on the look out for it.

Close below the fourth spring the river expands into a wide bed, full of watercress, brook-lime, and other aquatic plants, and at the lower end of this bed our river receives its first tributary, a little spring running from under the aqueduct of the canal. The bed of watercress has been noted for considerably more than a hundred years, and from here the stream meanders pleasantly through fertile fields, then hides itself under a long two-arched bridge, over which a road passes; above that being a branch line of the railway to Cirencester from Kemble Junction. Passing through some fields, the stream is again arched over by the road from Kemble to Ewen, where, making a sudden turn, it runs alongside the road, its banks being prettily shaded by trees and shrubs, under which in the season the sweet-scented violet grows, spreading its perfume in the soft evening air. So it glides into the little hamlet of Ewen, where many years ago our stream turned its first mill; and here too for the first time are its waters divided, a sluice being erected at the farm which stands in the place of the old mill. Past the sheep-washing place, the river dashes against the base of the hill; and, nearly buried in trees and bushes, hurries on with murmuring music to its next bridge, where with widening stream it flows through the open meadows; then by the side of a pleasant copse, and into the fields again.

A cut reaches from here, the original stream being only utilized to carry off the waste irrigation water; and soon we reach Somerford Upper Mill, now the first on the Thames, pleasantly shaded by elm trees, and in conjunction with the adjoining farm-buildings, forming a pretty picture. On some rising ground to the left is Somerford Keynes, in olden times the lordship of Ralph de Kaineto, who by marriage received this manor as a gift from Henry the First. In an ancient charter granted to the Abbot Aldelm of Malmesbury mention is made of certain lands here, and the river is named the Thames – 'Cujus vocabulum Temis juxta vadum qui appellatur Somerford'.

The square tower of the church, dedicated to All Saints, rises prettily above the trees, the white cottages peeping through and dotting the landscape. Then comes another mill, with house close by, a pleasant walk by the cool waters fringed with trees that lead up to a little bridge of stone, followed beyond by a modern brick mill, attached to a farm. The river here runs alongside a country road, and soon becoming broader, flows with softened stillness between the pleasant borders of an overhanging copse; and close to its brink runs a pretty pathway through the greenwood. Half a mile of this lovely strolling brings us past a quaint foot bridge, that forms the principal object in this exquisite picture of still life: it is supported by upright slabs of stone, which, broken and chipped on the surface, stand boldly up and give vigour to the subject. On past the Old Manor House of Ashton Keynes; the church, a little distance to the left, at the end of an avenue of trees: by the mill, and we are in the village (*Inn*, 'White Hart'), the stream making a sharp turn, running down by the side of the road in front of the houses. Ashton Keynes is remarkable for two things – the number of little bridges crossing the Thames, and the remains of four crosses in several parts of the village. Why so many were erected we have no record; but the church is dedicated to the Holy Cross. At the bottom of Ashton Keynes the Swill Brook enters our stream, which then by a short and winding course reaches Water Hay Bridge. In all probability the Thames was once navigable to this point for boats of 7 tons burden, which conveyed cheese, corn, etc., the produce of the county, to the storehouses still in existence below Lechlade, where they were reloaded into larger boats and sent to London and other towns down the river. This theory seems to be confirmed by the existing vestiges of several weirs at and above Cricklade; while the river would be fairly navigable for small boats as far as this place, were it not for obstructions, which are evidently of later date. However, be that as it may, the aqueduct of the North Wilts Canal, under which our river dives, with West Mill, and several barriers across the stream, effectually prevent the passage of any boat of burden; but it is quite possible, with an amount of labour in pulling over, etc., to force a small pleasure boat as far as Water Hay or even Oaklake Bridge. Nothing more to notice on our journey downwards till we arrive at Cricklade, which is generally at present the highest point reached by boats.

CRICKLADE

CRICKLADE BRIDGE to Oxford *43 miles 7 furlongs 2 yards; to London, (Putney Bridge) 148 miles 2 furlongs 68 yards*

Hotels – 'White Horse', 'White Hart'.
Railways – The Midland and South Western from Andover to Cirencester have a station (Cricklade) at the top of the High Street, but extremely few trains are run. GWR nearest station Purton (3 miles). Trains are met by omnibus some three times per day (fare *6d.*).

One of the best modes of reaching Cricklade is by rail to Lechlade (GWR), sending the boat to that station by carriage truck; the agent to the company will deliver the boat at Lechlade Wharf at a cost of 2s.; then rowing up to Inglesham Round House, and paying the toll (10s.), pass on to the canal through the Inglesham Lock (fall varies from 6 ft to 4 ft according to height of river). Six furlongs on is Dudgrove Double Lock, with its fall of 11 ft 6 in altogether, and then passing Kempsford it is 5½ miles to Eisey Lock (fall between 6 and 7 ft). The old lock-keeper will help through the first two locks, but a winch will be required at Eisey, there being no lock-keeper. In another mile and a half Cricklade Wharf is reached, and here, with the help of the wharfman, the boat can be carried across the road and lowered into the Churn, which runs by its side; then passing under the road bridge, a short distance brings us into the Thames a few yards above Rose Cottage, the owner of which is kind enough to allow boats to be left there.

Cricklade is an old quiet town, consisting mostly of one principal street. It boasts two churches, one, St Mary's, close to the river, a little old church, quiet and solemn, just like the town itself; the other, St Sampson, near the upper part of the street, a handsome cruciform edifice, with a beautiful square tower in the centre and in its interior open to a considerable height, and decorated with shields ornamented with armorial bearings, among which are those of the Nevilles and the Earls of Warwick. There are also two crosses, standing one in each churchyard, that near the lower church retaining its sculptured figures fairly intact. A little way below the bridge our river receives the waters of the Churn.

The good folk of Cricklade are blessed with a Waylands estate, which not only provides for the repair of the roads and pavements, but also lights up the streets with gas during the winter months without any rates to pay for it.

Leaving Rose Cottage, we pass under a curious plank bridge, just above which baptisms in the river used to be solemnized, a ceremony which has not taken place here for a number of years.

The river has been by the Thames Commissioners thoroughly dredged and cleaned out from some distance above Cricklade right down to Inglesham; the flams and shallows removed, so that now, in *fair water time*, it forms a continuous stream of something like 30 ft wide and 3 ft in depth. But this must not be taken to mean that the depth of water will always be found. On the contrary, the removal of the weeds and flams in all probability will, *during short water time*, allow the stream to waste so fast as to leave little to float even the shallowest draught of boat, and as far as oarsmen are concerned, effectually cut them off the river above Inglesham whenever the water is low, as the flams and rushes did in past summers.

CRICKLADE

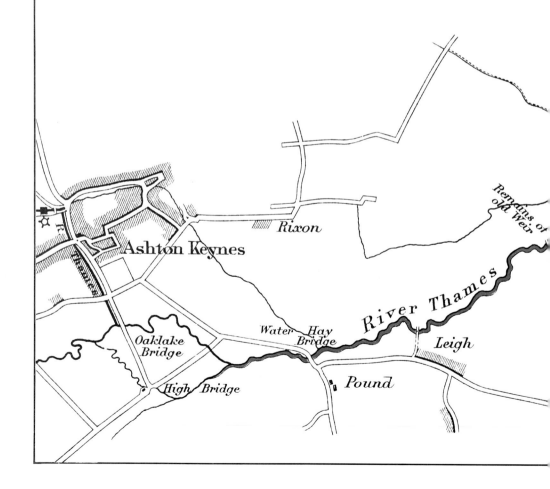

PLANK BRIDGE CRICKLADE

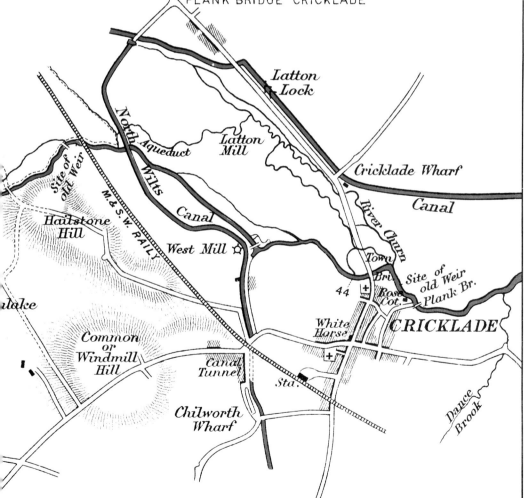

Latton
Lock

North Aqueduct

Latton
Mill

Site of
old Weir

Cricklade Wharf

Canal

M & S.W. RAIL.

Wilts

Hailstone
Hill

Canal

River Churn

West Mill

Town
Bri.

Site of
old Weir
Plank Br.

44

Ross
Cot.

lake

White
Horse

CRICKLADE

Common
or
Windmill
Hill

Canal
Tunnel

Sta.

Chilworth
Wharf

Dance
Brook

One more thing has been done by this same river cleansing. The banks are straightened, and along them is deposited mounds of earth, the *debris* of the stream, thoroughly taking out every bit of beauty, and giving the river the idea of a big ditch. The remains of the old weirs are entirely removed. Old picturesque bridges have now stiff substitutes; and anyone with an eye for the picturesque will be thoroughly disappointed with the bald appearance of the whole scene, except in a few cases which will be dealt with in their proper places. In two spots between Cricklade and Water Eaton Bridge we noticed posts had been driven into the bed of the stream, and a sharp look-out will have to be kept to avoid the danger of running on them in high water time, when the stream rushes down with great force, or if traversing the stream at night. Fishing will be at an end with no water in the river except where deep holes occur, and even these will no doubt be quickly denuded of their finny inhabitants the moment the water has shallowed.

For a short distance the stream is shaded by small trees, and when we reach Eisey footbridge we get a glimpse of Eisey Church, a small modern Norman edifice, half hidden in trees, on the rise of the hill. A fast crooked stream brings us to Water Eaton footbridge, in olden times narrow and difficult to get through against the rushing stream, now broadened and easy and new and straight. Below, at the turn, stands Water Eaton House, with its Elizabethan gables and mullioned windows; and here the river turns to the northward, soon reaching a kind of hook bend, the neck of which has been cut through and deepened, so that it forms the main stream, while the neglected part is fast silting and growing up. Then shortly follows Cow Neck, with its accompanying hollows, often filled with water. We have been unable to get at the origin of this curious place, and shall be glad to receive any information respecting it and its quaint name. The river now bends to the eastward, and soon passes the site of the Castle Eaton mill, no trace of which, however, remains; and then comes Castle Eaton, with its picturesque old bridge, one of the few remnants of the old, wild, half-deserted charm which the upper river used to possess.

CASTLE EATON

CASTLE EATON from Cricklade *4 miles 3 furlongs 178 yards; to Kempsford, 1 mile 4 furlongs 44 yards*

Inn – 'Red Lion'.

Castle Eaton has little to invite us to tarry. Its old bridge with broad rough piers, built with the stone of the district, and arched over by wooden beams, which carry the roadway, this and its combination with the church and cottages is a pretty subject for an artist. The old church with its square broad tower at the western end, and the pretty spirelet between nave and chancel, where once hung the *Sancte* bell, peeping through the foliage of the trees bordering the river, is, perhaps, the only remaining point of interest. How different in the past when the stream murmured through a rush-covered bed, often so high as to entirely hide the boat to its very mast pole, and right across the river as close as a well-grown field of standing corn. The rushes were a nuisance and a bother to oarsmen, but what pretty bits of foreground they helped to make!

Over the big meadow Kempsford church tower is seen, and the river meanders along towards it, approaching near to the canal before it finally turns to run past the remains of the old mansion of the great Dukes of Lancaster.

KEMPSFORD from Cricklade *6 miles 0 furlong 2 yards; to Inglesham Round House, 4 miles 5 furlongs*

Inn – 'George'. Land just below the farm.

Kempsford Church (dedicated to St Mary the Virgin), with its fine old tower, was mainly erected by Henry, Duke of Lancaster, in the fourteenth century; the remains of the mansion, consisting of a window with a piece of wall, being still visible on the river's bank.

Not far below Kempsford was the sill of an old weir, utilized by stepping stones as a way across the river in summer, but now entirely swept away by the new improvements which here, as in other places above and below, have lined the banks with mounds of soil dredged from the river. Our stream

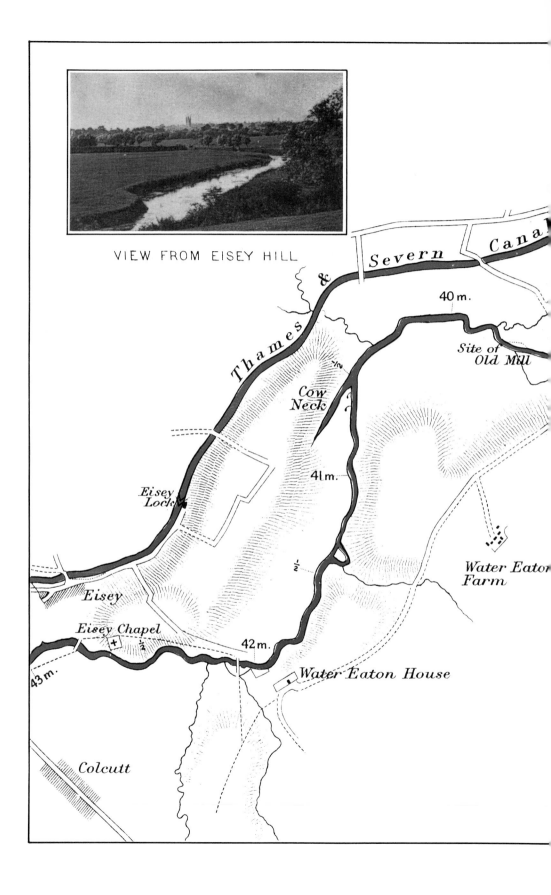

VIEW FROM EISEY HILL

Thames & Severn Canal

40 m.

Site of
Old Mill

Cow
Neck

41 m.

Eisey
Lock

Water Eaton
Farm

Eisey

Eisey Chapel

42 m.

43 m.

Water Eaton House

Colcutt

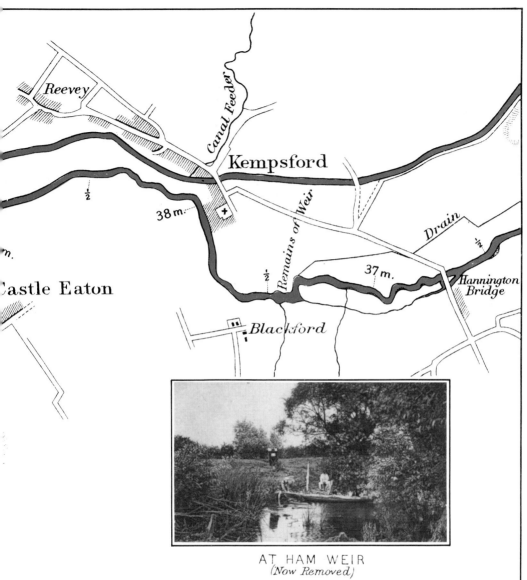

AT HAM WEIR
(Now Removed)

KEMPSFORD

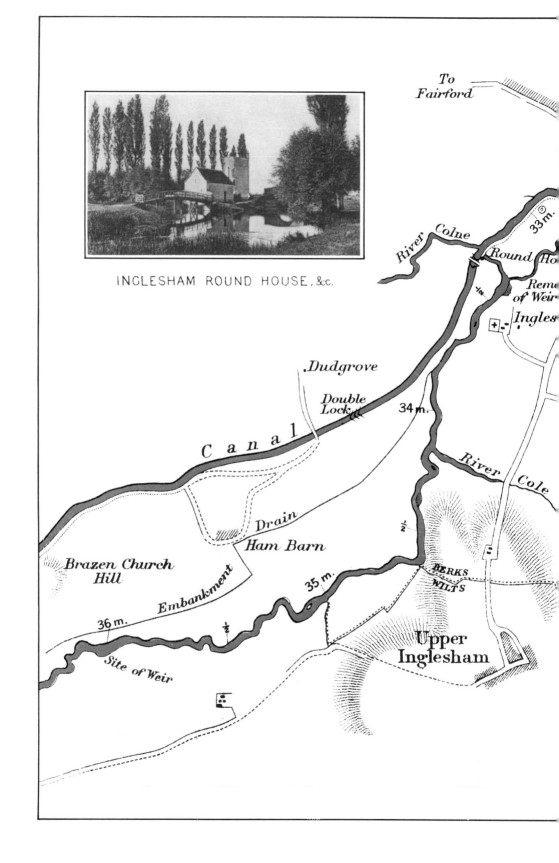

INGLESHAM ROUND HOUSE, &c.

To
Fairford

River Colne

33 m.

Round Ho

Rem
of Weir

Ingles

Dudgrove

Double
Lock

34 m.

C a n a l

River Cole

Drain

Ham Barn

Brazen Church
Hill

Embankment

BERKS
WILTS

35 m.

36 m.

Upper
Inglesham

Site of Weir

LECHLADE

Lechlade Mill

New Inn
Lechlade B.

½

St.John's
Bridge

Lower
Mill

Trout

Lock
32 m.

½

Willows

Site of
Old Stores

31 m.

½

30 m.

Buscot
Lock

Buscot

GLOSTERSHIRE

OXON

LECHLADE FROM THE RIVER

divides here, uniting again beyond Hannington Bridge, half a mile below which was the pretty bit of Ham Weir, the subject of one of our illustrations, but now entirely gone as if it never had existed. A couple of miles on and the little tributary the Cole enters the Thames, soon after which we come to Inglesham, with its old picturesque church, the bell-turret of which looks towards the river. In its wall is a curiosity that should not be passed unnoticed: a rude carving in stone of the Virgin and Child, and over them the semblance of a hand extended in the act of blessing.* Just below is the site of Inglesham Weir, for many years the highest up the Thames; and the river, passing through the old weir-pool, turns sharply to the left under the little wooden towing-path bridge, where it is joined by the Colne from Fairford and also the Thames and Severn Canal, the Round House belonging to the latter being close by. The Colne is noted for its trout, and at Fairford (from Lechlade 3¾ miles), the fishery being in the hands of the proprietor of the Bull Hotel, arrangements can be made for fishing either for a day or longer. Fairford is noted for the beautiful old glass in its church windows, supposed by some to have been from the designs of Albert Durer; the town was the birthplace of the Revd John Keble, the author of the *Christian Year*, etc.† From the Round House the breadth and depth of the river are greatly increased; once it was navigable along here for barges of 70 tons burden, drawing about 4 ft of water, but at the present time it would not be safe unless with high water in the river to depend upon getting any boat drawing more than 2 ft 6 in up as far as this.

A short reach from Inglesham brings us to Lechlade, where a boat can be left at the wharf close above the bridge.

* This carving is thought to be late Anglo-Saxon in date, the iconography deriving from Northumbrian sources, i.e., St Cuthbert's coffin, the *Book of Kells*.

† Revd John Keble (1792–1866). Educated at Oxford, he was Professor of Poetry there from 1831–41. His sermons on national apostasy in 1833 were considered the start of the Oxford Movement and his volume of sacred verse, *The Christian Year*, was universally admired. However, his preference was to live as the vicar of the country parish of Hursley from 1836–66. Keble College, Oxford, was founded in his memory in 1870.

LECHLADE

LECHLADE from Cricklade *11 miles 2 furlongs 134 yards; to St John's Lock 5 furlongs 88 yards*

Hotel – 'New Inn'.
Station – GWR (East Gloucestershire Branch) ½ mile from the town.

Lechlade is a small market town, quiet and dull, having nothing of interest excepting its church, a gem of Late Perpendicular work with a stone spire which harmonizes very gracefully with other details in several scenes from the river. One of the beauties of the interior is its chancel arch, which in combination each way with other arches springs from a light shaft in a most graceful way. Within the last few years this interior has been renovated, the old-fashioned sleeping boxes and gallery removed and replaced with light open pews, and the charming arcade of Gothic arches, dividing the nave from the aisles fully exposed to view. Perhaps the best way to reach Lechlade, if time be an object, is by rail (GWR); the stationmaster will arrange to convey the boat down to the wharf just above the bridge (see under Cricklade *ante*).

The Thames is crossed here by a stone bridge, having one large arch and two small ones, over which passes the road to Highworth, and 5 furlongs 88 yards below is St John's Lock, the first on the Thames.

ST JOHN'S LOCK to Buscot Lock *1 mile 1 furlong 50 yards; fall about 3 ft 6 in on an average.*

Inn – 'The Trout'.
St John's Bridge marks the site of a priory of Black canons, of which scarcely a vestige remains; one of the only remnants being a curious stone now in the possession of the Lord of the Manor (G. Milward, Esq.), found when digging close to the 'Trout Inn'. A little below, the River Lech, from which the town of Lechlade derives its name, falls into the Thames.

Fishing – The fishing is claimed by Mr Bower, of the 'Trout', who rents the water from the Inglesham Fishery to Eaton Hastings, but charges a nominal sum for rod and line. Sport should be good: jack, perch, roach, dace, chub,

HARTS WEIR

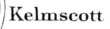

Kelmscott

29 m.

Harts Weir

Farm

28 m.

Remains of W

Eaton Hastings

RADCOT BRIDGE

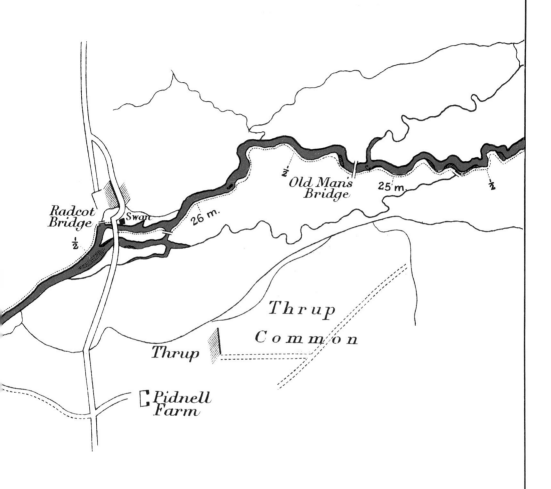

Radcot
Bridge

½

Swan

26 m.

Old Mans
Bridge

2

25 m.

½

Thrup
Common

Thrup

Pidnell
Farm

SIDE STREAM RADCOT

and barbel are plentiful, and in the pools of the weirs some fine trout are often to be found.

At St John's Bridge the navigation passes under a side arch, the weir taking up the centre one.

BUSCOT LOCK to Hart's Weir falls *(4 ft 6 in), 1 mile 2 furlongs 150 yards*

Just before reaching here we pass the site of the immense factory where spirit was made from beetroot; the manufacture not being successful has been given up and the factory entirely taken down.

HART'S WEIR from Lechlade Bridge *3 miles 1 furlong 68 yards; to Radcot Bridge 3 miles 0 furlongs 140 yards*

Inn – No beds.

Hart's Weir has the greatest fall (nearly 4 ft sometimes in low water) of any among the weirs of the upper Thames, so perhaps a word or two upon passing through would not be out of place. In winter there is a swift stream through, but very little fall, the weir-paddles being all out; and the only thing to guard against in shooting is the bridge that carries the rymers. I recollect one winter in passing this very weir, when lying on my back in the boat to get through, scraping a fair amount of skin off my nose and face, through contact with the bridge whilst going under. In summer there is no fear of that, as the bridge is a long way above the water; but what must be looked out for is, the nearly direct fall of a foot or more in ascending or descending, and this perhaps in a spot only just wide enough to get a boat through. Weirs are built in a very different way from locks, and, to a person not used to them, are rather puzzling. They take up the whole breadth of the stream, so that in opening them fully, you let the whole of the penned-back water above pass through; they are generally composed of three different parts, viz., the bridge, the rymers, and the paddles. The bridge is longer than the span of the stream it has to cover, and works round on a pin; the part on the shore-side being weighted to balance the other, and notches cut to let the rymers in and keep each one in its place. On the sill, at the bottom of the river, exactly underneath the bridge, are corresponding sockets to hold their ends, and then the paddles fill up the spaces between each; the weight of the water above keeping all tight. Generally, for small boats, only a few of the paddles and rymers are moved, so that there is always a fall, and the best way to get up is to fasten your tow-line to the head of the boat, and gently haul her, one person being on the bridge of the weir to guide her through. As a rule, unless the weir is all out, you will not get through by any other way. Going down is different, and much easier, though somewhat dangerous (most of the weir-pools being very deep); but, having ascertained that everything is ready, pull gently on, and keep your boat's head *straight* to the centre of the opening, just before reaching which the oars must be shifted, yet kept ready to be used again the moment you are past, as the stream rushing through causes a strong back-current. It is always better, if you have not been through before, to get help from the neighbouring cottage, refreshing yourself, if needed; and a small quantity of the Englishman's *bucksheesh* (beer) will always find you a willing assistant. Sometimes it is wiser, and saves time, to drag the boat over (if you can), rather than pass through; but this must be a matter for consideration at the time.

RADCOT BRIDGE from Hart's Weir *3 miles 0 furlong 140 yards; to Rushy Lock, 3 miles 1 furlong 210 yards*

Inn – 'Swan'.
Station – Faringdon Station, GWR branch, 2 miles right.
Radcot Bridge, a structure of three Gothic arches, is interesting from its historical associations, having been the scene of more than one battle. In 1387, Robert de Vere, Earl of Oxford, was defeated here by the refractory barons under the command of Henry of Derby, afterwards Henry the Fourth. De Vere escaped by swimming the river on his horse. A skirmish also took place here in the Civil Wars; the bridge, being fortified as an outwork to Faringdon House, was taken by Cromwell's troops, but, although successful so far, they could not reduce the fortified mansion at Faringdon Hill. In the centre of the old bridge are traces of the cross that once ornamented it, the socket in which the upright stone was inserted still remaining. The banks in the autumn used in places to be lined with luxuriant beds of watercresses, but we are unable to say what effect present dredging will have upon them.

   We pass a footbridge at Old Man's, marking the site of a weir, and a little more than a mile below the site of another weir which when in existence was

TADPOLE BRIDGE

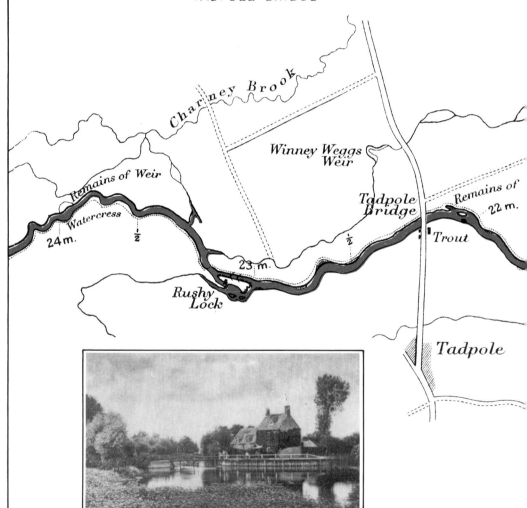

RUSHY WEIR

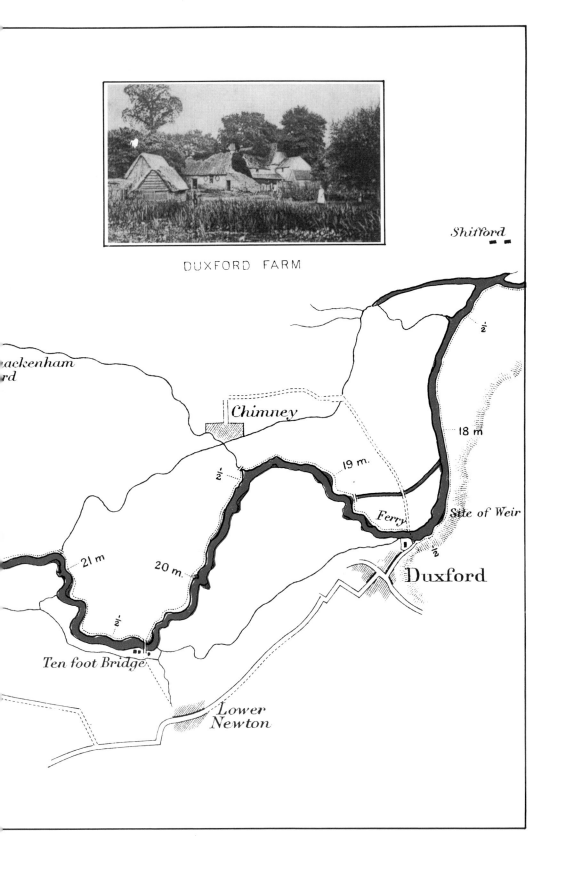

DUXFORD FARM

Shifford

ackenham
rd

Chimney

½

½

19 m.

18 m.

Ferry

Site of Weir

21 m

20 m.

½

Duxford

½

½

Ten foot Bridge

Lower
Newton

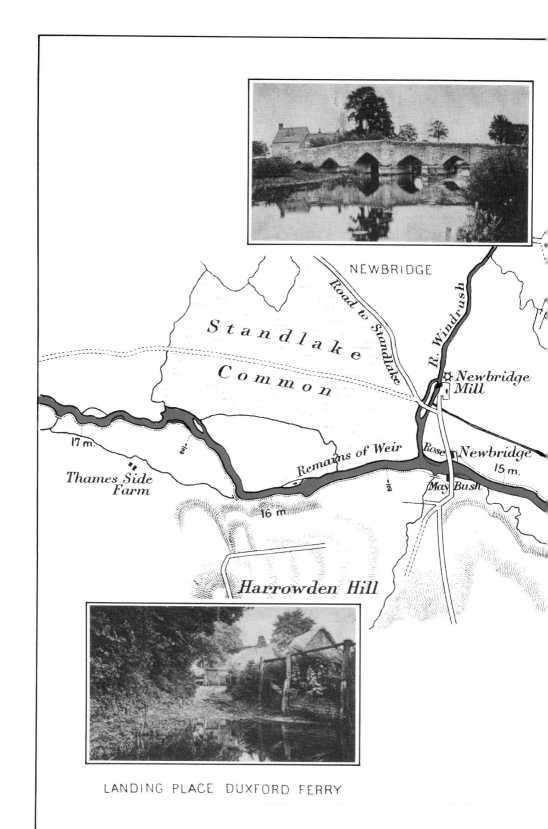

NEWBRIDGE

Road to Standlake

S t a n d l a k e

C o m m o n

R. Windrush

☼ *Newbridge Mill*

17 m.

2½

Thames Side Farm

Remains of Weir

Rose

Newbridge

15 m.

½

May Bush

16 m

Harrowden Hill

LANDING PLACE DUXFORD FERRY

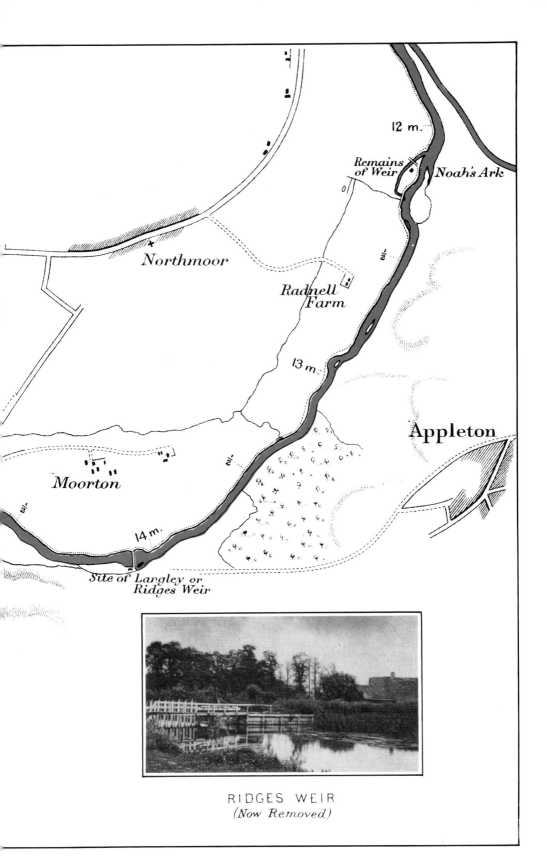

12 m.

Remains
of Weir

Noah's Ark

0

½

Northmoor

Radnell
Farm

13 m.

Appleton

Moorton

14 m.

Site of Largley or
Ridges Weir

RIDGES WEIR
(Now Removed)

Rushy Weir and lock house c. 1887

called Old Nan's, of which no trace remains; then half a mile onwards come Rushy Lock and Weir – the lock fall being about 2 ft 6 in.

Rushy is a charming picture, formed by the old weir with the fine pool below the bridge nearly shut in with trees and guarded by the lock house embosomed in foliage; the foreground crammed with weeds and river parsley; its loveliness enhanced by the murmuring music of the water as it ripples over the paddles of the weir.

Fishing – The fishing here is in the hands of Townsend at the weir house. A variety of fish in the pool and in the deeps formed by the eddies of the stream – big perch and roach, jack, chub, eels, and some trout.

TADPOLE BRIDGE a short mile below. From Lechlade *10 miles 2 furlongs 154 yards; to Ten-Foot bridge 1 mile 6 furlongs 154 yards*

Inn – The 'Trout', close to the bridge and by the side of the road; this little inn has fair accommodation.

Fishing – The fishing from Rushy Weir to Ten-Foot bridge, is in the hands of the landlord of the 'Trout' Inn. He strictly preserves this water, but it is open to his customers for angling. The water is rented from Sir W. Throckmorton, who is the owner and lord of the manor. A variety of fish are to be found, amongst them some good trout, eels, jack, fine perch, roach and chub, the latter in great profusion.

Below Tadpole is a dreary winding stretch of river lined with straight flood banks on either side, between which when the water is high the stream is penned. In no other place on the Thames are floods more frequent than here, and even when the river is well between its banks the swampy sides have no attractions.

Ten-Foot bridge, the site of an old weir, follows, and here the river tends northward, passing the hamlet of Chimney, and then turns to the southward towards Duxford Farm and landing place. An old weir once existed just below; and then another mile brings us past Shifford, which according to a MS in the Cottonian Library had the honour of being the place where a Parliament assembled in the reign of Alfred the Great. One more old weir pool, called after the old Standlake Fisherman Daniels', and a short mile brings us to the mouth of the Windrush, just above Newbridge.

The River Windrush is a curious stream, rising in the Cotswolds. It runs its course with many a twist and curve past the villages and towns of Bourton-on-

Bablock Hythe ferry c. 1875

the-Water, Burford, and Witney. Between the two latter places, its nitrous waters help to give the far-famed Witney blankets the superiority they claim over all others of the same class of manufacture. It is not navigable, and the lower part of the stream is not worth exploring.

NEWBRIDGE from Tadpole *6 miles 7 furlongs 208 yards; to Ridge's Bridge 1 mile 1 furlong 62 yards*

The *oldest* bridge on the Thames, built some 600 years ago by the monks of an abbey which then existed here. An inn on either side of the bridge, the 'May Bush' on the Berkshire and the 'Old Rose Revived' on the Oxfordshire bank, but they do not afford much accommodation. A skirmish took place here on 27 May 1664, resulting in the defeat of a party of the Parliamentarians, who retired to Abingdon, and revenged themselves by destroying the beautiful cross which then stood in the market place.

The bridge has six pointed arches, with ribs strengthening them, a narrow roadway and bold piers which open to the road, and form places of refuge from passing vehicles for foot passengers.

Fishing – The fishing above Newbridge is scarcely as good as below, although there are spots which repay the angler for his toil as in the old weir pool at Daniels', for instance, or along the reach leading up to Duxford, where there are several likely spots easily noted by the practised hand.

RIDGE'S BRIDGE from Newbridge *1 mile 1 furlong 62 yards; to Bablock Hythe Ferry, 2 miles 4 furlongs 70 yards*

A new bridge, comes next, the river expanding into a fine reach, bordered on one side by pollard willows, while the other is fringed with high reeds like parts of the Warwickshire Avon and other streams. No inn, but two beds here; and the water is preserved by different owners from Newbridge down to past Skinner's Bridge some 5 miles below, making in all about 7 miles of preserved water in which abound the usual class of Thames fish, with the addition of now and then a spotted trout. A pleasant smiling reach of 2 miles brings us to the remains of Ark Weir, with its fine perch fishing; and in half a mile we reach Bablock Hythe Ferry (from Skinner's Weir, 1 mile 5 furlongs 34 yards): (*Inn*, 'The Chequers') 5 miles from Oxford by road. Two miles by

EYNSHAM BRIDGE

SKINNERS WEIR
(Now Removed)

BABLOCK HYTHE FERRY

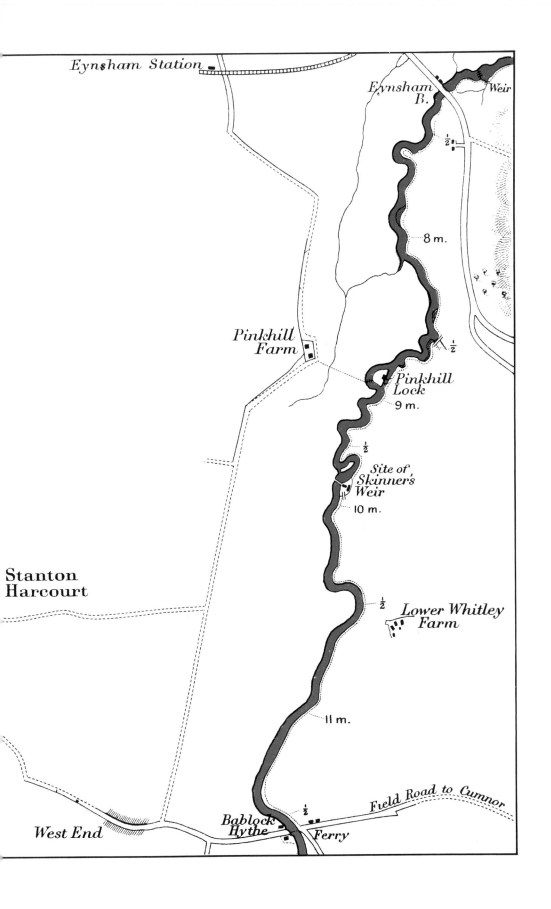

Eynsham Station

Eynsham B.

Weir

½

8 m.

Pinkhill Farm

½

Pinkhill Lock

9 m.

½

Site of Skinner's Weir

10 m.

Stanton Harcourt

½

Lower Whitley Farm

11 m.

½

Field Road to Cumnor

West End

Bablock Hythe

Ferry

road (left) is Stanton Harcourt (*Inn*, 'Harcourt Arms'), with its old house and kitchen, and also a fine cruciform church dating from the twelfth century. In one of the rooms of a tower belonging to the Manor House, Pope is stated to have finished his translation of the Fifth Book of Homer's *Iliad*. On our way there we pass the 'Devil's Coits', three large stones reared in three fields supposed to commemorate a battle fought in Saxon times.

On the hill on the Berks side of the Ferry is Cumnor (1½ miles), made famous in Sir Walter Scott's *Kenilworth*. No part of the mansion remains; but the church, picturesquely shaded by trees, and containing amongst others the tomb of Antony Forster, is worth visiting. *Inn*, 'Bear and Ragged Staff' (not the original one mentioned in *Kenilworth*). No reach on the Upper Thames contains so much water as this one kept up by Pinkhill Lock; and it is usually from this point that the flashes or flushes which help boats down the stream in low water time are begun.

SKINNER'S BRIDGE Late Skinner's Weir from Bablock Hythe Ferry *1 mile 5 furlongs 34 yards; to Pinkhill Lock, 1 mile*

This is one of the new gallows bridges which have taken the place of the old weirs. The old weir, with its couple of quaint thatched cottages, was one of those picturesque places that artists love. It had been in the possession of the Skinners from father to son for a long number of years. It was a little inn, and the last landlord, Joe Skinner, was one of the best hearted, quaintest fellows that ever lived. He was original in the highest degree, and it was a rich treat to spend an evening with him and listen to his talk of havoc wrought among the wild ducks, with his stalking horse and tremendous duck gun, or his curious remarks on someone who had been there, and, not understanding him, had rubbed old Joe the wrong way of the wool, getting perhaps a rough setting down. This is all swept away by the march of improvement: the old cottages, the tumbledown weir, and old Joe are all gone, and the place entirely lone and deserted. This is the nearest point to Stanton Harcourt, which lies a short mile across the fields. Below here the windings of the river for the next 2 miles appear like the contortions of a dying serpent, in places nearly doubling on itself and making the distance twice as long as it otherwise would be, with the additional disadvantage a sharp stream with sudden bends always gives to an oarsman rowing up.

PINKHILL (or Pinkle) LOCK from Skinner's *1 mile; to Eynsham Bridge, 1 mile 4 furlongs 27 yards: falls 3 ft on an average*

Has been rebuilt within the last few years, a cottage added for the lock-keeper, and a new big weir, but has nothing beside to be noticed, and we pass on round the numerous windings of the river to Eynsham Bridge.

EYNSHAM or Swynford Bridge to King's Weir *2 miles 6 furlongs 161 yards*

A private toll bridge, built some eighty or ninety years ago by the late Earl of Abingdon to replace the old ford. Eynsham village is distant about half a mile to the left.

Station – GWR; Witney Branch.
Inns – 'Swan', 'Red Lion'; once had a celebrated abbey of which few traces now remain. The boat can be left at the bridge in charge of Treadwell, the river and weir-keeper. Just below is Eynsham or Boldes Weir, now (1886) in a ruinous state, but will, in due course, be rebuilt or else done away with, as the Conservators are improving the river in every way but the picturesque. The river sweeps along the base of the Wytham Hills which here spring up to their greatest elevation, and we pass the mouth of the Evenlode, a tributary rising near Moreton-in-Marsh, Cassington Spire being a notable object a short distance from the river. Nothing further to notice till King's Weir is reached, where the river divides, the stream to the left leading to Duke's Lock where the Oxford Canal is joined. The latter is the best way perhaps to take a steam launch or any large boat which cannot be pulled over, down to Oxford (toll 2s. 6d.), as the weir is difficult to open; ordinary boats are pulled over the boat slide at the right-hand side of the weir.
Fishing – The fishing from Skinner's Weir to Godstow is mostly owned by the Earl of Abingdon, who has let the angling above King's Weir to the Oxford Angling and Preservation Society (hon. secretary, W. Kelson). The water from King's Weir to Godstow is in the hands of the proprietor of the 'Trout' Inn, Godstow, who arranges for the fishing with his customers.

There is very fair fishing in some parts of this stretch of water. Chub and barbel are taken at the weirs, jack and perch are in the deeps, while roach and dace are nearly everywhere, with now and then a few trout.

Below Godstow, the fishing is very poor, the pleasure traffic being

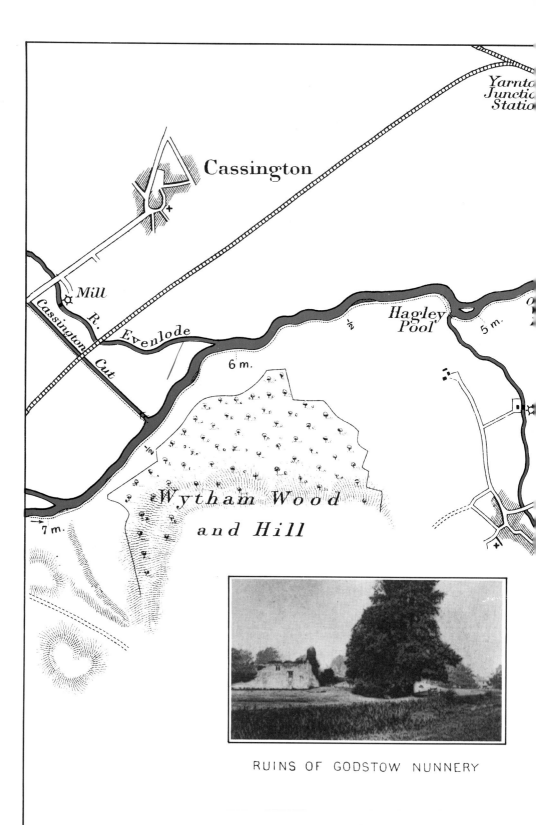

Yarnton
Junction
Station

Cassington

Mill

Cassington Cut

R. Evenlode

Hagley
Pool

½

5 m.

6 m.

½

7 m.

½

Wytham Wood
and Hill

RUINS OF GODSTOW NUNNERY

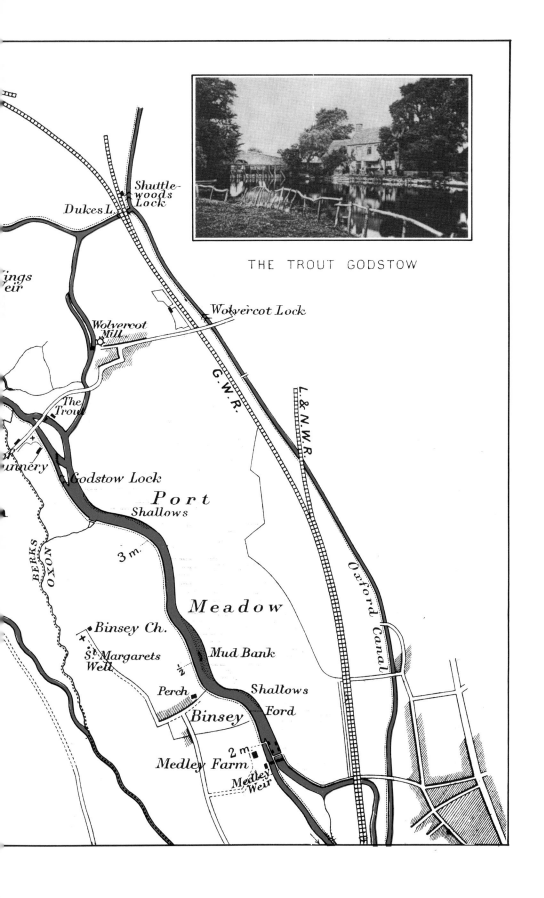

THE TROUT GODSTOW

Shuttle-
woods
Lock

Dukes L.

'ings
'eir

Wolvercot Lock

Wolvercot
Mill

G.W.R.

L & N.W.R.

The
Trout

'h
'unnery

Godstow Lock

Port

Shallows

3 m.

BERKS
OXON

Meadow

•Binsey Ch.

St. Margarets
Well

Mud Bank

½

Perch

Shallows

Binsey

Ford

Oxford Canal

2 m.

Medley Farm

Medley
Weir

extensive, and except at Medley Weir, there is perhaps hardly a spot that is worth the time and trouble of a pitch.

Fisherman – Richard Tredwell, Eynsham.

King's Weir to Godstow Lock, 1 mile 1 furlong 153 yards (falls 3 ft 6 in), has lately been greatly enlarged, the old house pulled down, and the river below cleared. Just above it is the new intake of water to supply the City of Oxford. Wolvercot Mill, where the paper for the Oxford Bibles is manufactured,* lies on the back stream, its tall chimney attracts attention, and then comes Godstow Bridge, with its picturesque little inn ('The Trout'), prettily situated on the edge of the side weir pool, and just below, the old Abbey.

GODSTOW

The remains of the abbey and convent of Godstow are situated on the island formed by the side stream running past Wytham, and close to the navigable cut of the river in which is situated Godstow Lock (from Medley Weir, 1 mile 3 furlongs 63 yards: fall 3 ft (lock-keeper). *Be careful of the Weir in high water.* The place is interesting from its connection with Fair Rosamond,† who was educated and afterwards buried here, and who, probably, spent the last few years of her life in seclusion within these walls, the commonly received story of the poisoned chalice forced on her by the jealous Queen Eleanor not having any foundation in fact. The actual circumstances are so folded in a network of fiction that it is difficult to disentangle them; but it seems probable that when receiving her education here, she was seen and loved by Prince Henry, then at Oxford, and, yielding to his guidance, was protected by him until his marriage with Eleanor of Guienne, when she retired again to the convent. Her remains were interred before the high altar,

---

* In 1857 a new papermill was built replacing an older mill, to develop and extend the University's right to print Bibles and Prayer Books. It specialized in making bible-paper with its particular characteristics of thinness and opacity. In 1865 the annual production was one million books.

† 'Fair Rosamond' was the daughter of Walter, Lord Clifford, and the mistress of Henry II by whom she had two sons. Henry built her a house in Godstow where she could live secretly, but the story tells that she was discovered by the jealous Queen Eleanor and poisoned. It is thought, however, that she retired to Godstow Nunnery to end her days.

the spot being marked by a costly and beautiful tomb, which – according to Higden – was lavishly decorated by Henry. In 1191, Hugh, Bishop of Lincoln, when visiting the place, in a very harsh manner caused the body to be removed; but after a while, the sisterhood collected the desecrated bones and laid them, enclosed in a perfumed leather bag, in the abbey church again, where they were found so preserved after the suppression of the nunnery. The existing vestiges are but few; the chapter house, close to the river, unroofed and partly overgrown with ivy, being the only building; but the walls yet standing round a spacious area give a fair idea of its former extent. The buildings, which were used as barracks during the civil war, were for the most part consumed by a disastrous fire. Passing through the Lock, we are in the main river again, and a pleasant row of a mile brings us to Binsey village on the towing-path side (*Inn*, 'The Perch'); the other bank being formed by Port Meadow, a fine open mead presented by William the Conqueror to the citizens of Oxford as a free common, and as such preserved. Being very liable to floods, caused partly by the silting up of the river, the meadow during such times is covered with all descriptions of craft. Una-boat sailing being especially enjoyed when the depth of water is sufficient, whilst in case of a frost a magnificent sheet of ice is formed, which, being thoroughly safe, yields to the inhabitants of Oxford a great pleasure. Binsey Church is a very small old structure about half a mile from the village; close by which was the noted well of St Margaret which the prayers of St Frideswyde caused to be opened, and it was held in such repute as to bring together a large multitude of pilgrims, who were provided for in the twenty-four inns the place then contained. A bridge is stated to have stretched across the river here; but no trace of it is to be seen. Medley, just below, had also a religious sanctuary belonging to Osney Abbey.

MEDLEY WEIR from Godstow Lock *1 mile 3 furlongs 63 yards; to Oxford (Folly Bridge), 1 mile 7 furlongs; falls from 1 ft 6 in to 2 ft in summer, open in high water time (weir-keeper)*

Boats Housed and to Let – J. Beesley, Medley Weir; W. Bossom, Medley Weir; Theo. Smith, Medley Weir

The river divides at Medley, the old navigable stream which many years ago led past the remains of Rewley Abbey to the city is now nearly grown up; the navigation is down the straight stream, and below the Weir we come to the

The Thames at Medley, Oxford, showing the landing stages of the boat building and hiring firms of William Bossom and G. Beesley c. 1880

'Four Streams', the right-hand one forming the fine public bathing-place of 'Tumbling Bay'; that to the left, passing under the railway bridges to Louse Lock, the connection with the Oxford Canal.

We soon after pass under Seven Bridges Road, close by being the GWR and L & NW Railway (Oxford) Stations.

The bridge was the scene of an accident on 2 December 1885, part of one of the piers and the centre arch giving way and carrying with it some four or five persons into the rushing stream, one of whom was drowned. A short distance brings us to Osney Lock (in high water be careful of the weir just above it on the towing path bank); close by stood Osney Abbey, once among the most magnificent in England, now represented by a gateway and little piece of wall in which is a perpendicular window of two lights built into part of the Mill. Osney Lock (to Oxford Bridge 7 furlongs: falls 6 ft), has lately been rebuilt and below we pass under the main line of the GWR, then past the Oxford Gas Works, now extended to both banks of the river, and a very short distance brings us to Folly Bridge, and we are amongst the barges and boats which make the river here so interesting and gay when crowded with people in their brightest costume on the occasion of the Procession of Boats on Commemoration Monday.

OXFORD

Oxford is, more often than any other place, the starting-point for a long Thames trip, and is one of the best places for that purpose, as every convenience is there to be met with.

Dean Stanley* speaks of Oxford as a mass of towers, pinnacles, and spires, rising from the bosom of a valley, from groves which hide all buildings but such as are consecrated to some wise and holy purpose; and it is perhaps – if a day can be spared – a wise plan to run down by rail and spend it here, among the beautiful specimens of collegiate architecture which give a semi-ecclesiastical air to the city; a trip which will be more than repaid by the pleasure which will be derived from the visit; and as Oxford is one of the most

---

* Arthur Penrhyn Stanley (1815–81) was Dean of Westminster. He studied Classics at Oxford and was appointed Secretary of the Oxford University Commission. He was chosen by Queen Victoria to accompany the Prince of Wales on his Eastern Tour in 1862.

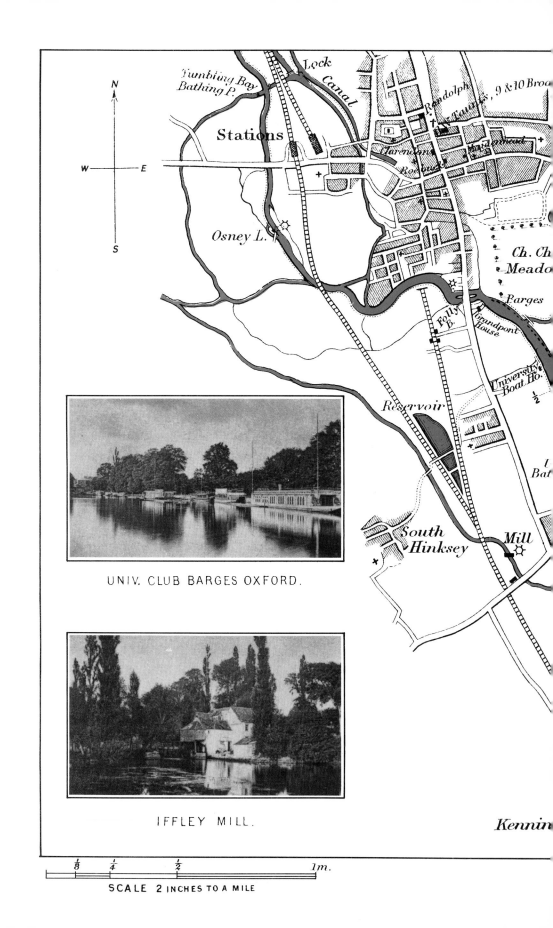

Tumbling Bay
Bathing P.

Lock

Canal

Randolph

9 & 10 Broa

Stations

Clarendon

Maidenhead

Roebuck

Osney L.

Ch. Ch
Mead

Parges

Folly
B.

Grandpont
House

University
Boat Ho.

½

Reservoir

Bat

South
Hinksey

Mill

Kennin

UNIV. CLUB BARGES OXFORD.

IFFLEY MILL.

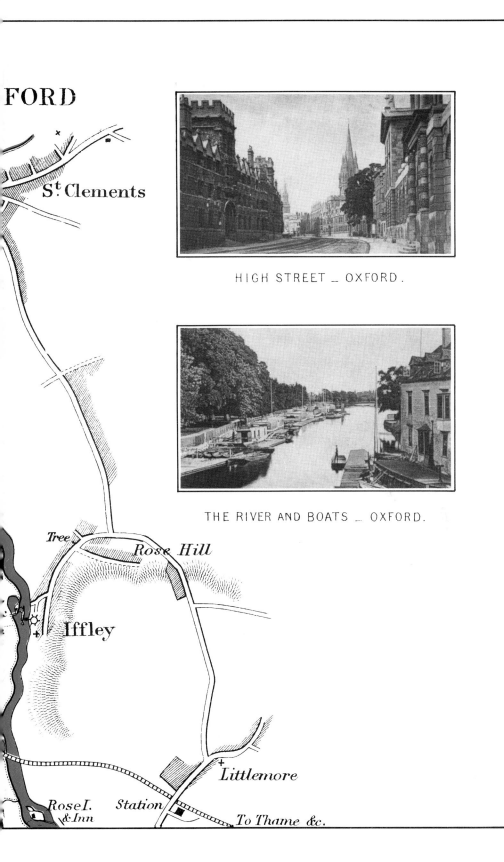

FORD

St Clements

HIGH STREET — OXFORD.

THE RIVER AND BOATS — OXFORD.

Tree

Rose Hill

Iffley

Littlemore

Rose I.
& Inn

Station

To Thame &c.

OXFORD.

RANDOLPH HOTEL,

IN THE CENTRE OF THE CITY.

THE only modern built Hotel in Oxford, close to the Colleges and Public Buildings, and commanding a fine open view down Beaumont Street, St. Giles's Street, and Magdalen Street, opposite

THE MARTYRS' MEMORIAL.

Handsome Suites of Apartments. Drawing Room, Billiard Rooms, and every modern comfort and convenience.
Excellent Wines imported direct from abroad.

CHARGES MODERATE.

GOOD STABLING AND LOOSE BOXES.

Visitors at this Hotel will meet with every attention and consideration.

Address—THE MANAGER.

noted spots on the river, not to have seen it is to have missed a huge treat. Information of every description required, guide books, guides, photographs, or letterpress views, can be readily obtained from Henry W. Taunt & Co.'s well-known establishment, 9 and 10, Broad Street, Oxford; the proprietors of which lay themselves out to furnish strangers to the city with any needed help.

Oxford is connected with London by two railway lines: the Great Western from Paddington (63 miles; fares 11s., 8s. 4d., and Par. 5s. 3d.), on which run the best fast trains; and the London and North-Western from Euston Station (78 miles; fares as from Paddington). The stations for both lines are close together at the bottom of Park End Street, cabs and 'buses meet each train, and a new line of tramways from just outside each railway station leads up the main streets of the City.

The Post Office is a fine new building in St Aldate's Street (leading to Folly Bridge and the river), where letters can be posted for London till 12 midnight, the office being open for inquiries, etc., on week days from 6.30 a.m. till 10 p.m., and on Sundays from 7 a.m. till 10 a.m.

The majority of the collegiate and public buildings in Oxford are open to the public during certain hours without any fee, and even to those where a fee is required, it is in every case so small as to be quite nominal. A week can easily be spent in Oxford by anyone fond of architectural beauty, but a glance round can be made in a day; and the author of this work is now engaged on a Guide to Oxford so arranged as to lead to all the salient points in a day, or going into details over which the week may well be spent. The following slight outline may be followed with advantage, starting from Carfax (the centre of the City): –

Down St Aldate's Street to Christ Church, across the Quadrangle to Dining Hall, Cathedral, and through the Cloisters to the Meadow Buildings and Broad Walk; back through Cloisters, Tom Quad, to Peckwater Quad and Canterbury Gate.

Note Corpus Christi College and Merton Tower, then across to Oriel Quadrangle, up Oriel Lane to St Mary's Church and Porch.

Down the High, past All Souls' College (l), University College (r), Queen's College (l), New Schools (r), to Magdalen College and its beautiful Tower.

Enter College at New Gate, under Cloisters to New Buildings and Water Walks, return through Cloisters (see Chapel if wished), and again into the High.

Across the road to Botanic Gardens (if wished), view of Merton Fields, Magdalen Bridge, etc.

Back up High Street, note different views with unfolding curve, turn up

Oxford. Queen's College barge during the College Eights c. 1890

New College Street, passing St Edmund's Hall (*r*). St Peter's in the East Church: under archway to New College, which enter. See Quadrangle with Chapel and Hall (*r*), Garden Quadrangle and Gardens, with old City Wall beyond, and then visit Chapel and Cloister Quadrangle.

Thence continuing up New College Street to Theatre and Clarendon Buildings, pass Hertford College to Radcliffe Library and Square; note Brasenose College, All Souls' Sister Towers, and then through passage into Schools Quadrangle and Bodleian Library (door to *l*). Pass on through Schools to Theatre, Ashmolean Museum, and thence crossing Broad Street, up Park Street to Wadham College, the Museum, and Keble College.

Through a side street into St Giles', turn down to St John's, enter, see Cloister Quadrangle and Gardens, back across to Martyrs' Memorial, Taylor Buildings, Randolph Hotel, down Beaumont Street to Worcester College if wished, and on into Broad Street.

Note † in road where Martyrs supposed to have been burnt; and close by, Henry W. Taunt & Co.'s establishment (where rest if wished).

Note Balliol College, Trinity College (both *l*), then turning down Turl Street, Exeter College (*l*) with its beautiful Chapel, Jesus College (*r*), and Lincoln College, with All Saint's Church beyond.

This will again lead into the top part of the High Street and Carfax, and you will have glanced at the greater part of the lions of Oxford. We have not yet noticed the river, although one of the greatest beauties of Oxford, as Oarsmen and River Tourists, for whom our book is written, will make that their chief study as they pass on their journey down its waters; but we may mention that its gayest time is during the May races, or on the grand occasion of the Procession of Boats* which takes place annually on the evening of Monday in Commemoration Week, when the river is alive with an endless variety of pleasure boats, and the gay barges are made gayer by the joyous crowds which throng them and the river's bank.

---

* The Procession of Boats ceremony consisted of the Head Boat (which had won first place in the Autumn Eights) being stationed to receive the honour of 'tossing of oars' from each of the other boats as they passed by. 'Many of the crew stood up and raised the bulk of their oars to their shoulders with the blades in the air, and although this can easily be done, and safely, it was often made the excuse to upset, and in a trice the boat would be over and the crew larking about in the water. Of course this joke increased the excitement and if properly carried out was very effective adding largely to the scene which sometimes grew a shade monotonous and tame.' – Henry Taunt.

Oxford. Downstream from Folly Bridge with many different types of boats in view including the college barges moored against the river bank c. 1875

The Torpid Races in the Lent Term and the Eights in the May Term are among the grandest specimens of eight-oared boat races, and few can escape the enthusiasm with which the racing boats are escorted up by their partisans. The scene is a stirring one, and well worth a visit, as the College Eights, some twenty or more in number, each one striving to catch and bump the one above (when it takes its place), race up the river from Iffley, excited to the utmost by the shouts and roar from their comrades on the towing path, as well as by the gay crowds assembled on the barges to see them come in. The barges on the river at Oxford are used by the different University boating clubs as lounges, dressing rooms, etc.; they are unequalled anywhere for number and beauty; many of their predecessors were the old London barges belonging to the various City companies, which have here found a last resting-place.

Boating is a very favourite pastime at Oxford; the river during term is always well furnished with boats of every class, and in the Long Vacation a City Regatta also takes place on Bank Holiday in August, which is usually well attended.

Hotels – The 'Randolph', Beaumont Street; The 'Roebuck', Cornmarket; The 'Clarendon', Cornmarket; The 'Mitre', High Street; The 'Golden Cross', Cornmarket; The 'King's Arms', Holywell.

Restaurants – J. Boffin, 107 High Street; F. Flight, Carfax.

Among the tradesmen we may mention Messrs Henry W. Taunt & Co., Broad Street, well known for their beautiful photographs of Oxford and the scenery of the Thames, as well as their manufactures of Oxford, Early English, and other characteristic styles of picture frames and fancy oak work; Messrs Spiers & Son, High Street, noted for articles suitable for presents from Oxford; E.C. Alden, Oxford guides, photographs, &c., Cornmarket; Messrs Foster & Co., in the High Street and Mr C.R. Ridley, St Aldate's, for boating uniforms and requisites for boating men and visitors; and J. Thornton & Son, Broad Street, for books.

OXFORD FOLLY BRIDGE from Lechlade *32 miles 4 furlongs 88 yards; to London Bridge, 111 miles 5 furlongs 66 yards; to Iffley Lock, 1 mile 3 furlongs 150 yards*

This was till 1885 the site of an old lock and weir, now entirely removed. This present bridge was preceded by an old one, consisting of a number of pointed arches, and on the island in the centre it was embellished with a curious

Sandford-on-Thames. The King's Arms Hotel with the paper mill and lock viewed from the tow-path c. 1875

building, under which the road passed, which was used by the celebrated Friar Bacon, and called after him 'Friar Bacon's Study'.* Here begin the College Barges, which make the scene from the bridge and also the river so extremely interesting, and among them are a variety of smaller boats.

Boats to be Let and Housed – J. Salter, Folly Bridge and at Barge; R.A. Talboys, Ch. Ch. Meadow, lower end; T. Tims, O.U. Boathouse and O.U. Barge; W. Crissall, Brasenose Barge and Isis Street; F. Rough, Folly Bridge and the Long Bridges.

Watermen – T. Tims, G. Hicks, W. Hicks, W. Parrott, W. Taylor, G. Best, H. Blagrove, W. Langford, J. Round, C. Robbins, C. Blagrove, C. Castle, J. Bossom, A. Beesley, S. Beesley, T. Barnes, T. Harris, W. Crissall, W. Round, R. Gibbs, D. Talboys, W. Gibbons.

Fishermen – W. Bossom, Medley Weir, C. Cook, T. Harris.

Bathing – Parson's Pleasure, at the back of the Parks; Tumbling Bay, near the Stations; New University, at the Long Bridges.

Library – There is a fine FREE Public Library under the Town Hall, in St Aldate's Street.

Leaving Oxford on the journey downwards, we pass the Barges we have before mentioned, and between them is the old mouth of the River Cherwell, which rising at Cherwell House, in Northamptonshire, here joins the Thames. A new mouth has lately been cut not far below, to relieve the Cherwell in flood time, and the stream for some distance has been cleared out. This river, although not navigable, is easily passable for pleasure boats, along the side of the beautiful Christ Church and Magdalen Water Walks, for some distance; and it is possible for those who do not mind difficulties to force a small boat as far as Islip, some 6 or 7 miles up its stream. Opposite the new cut is the picturesque University Boat House. A quarter of a mile lower down the new Thames are the Long Bridges, with F. Rough's Boat House just above. Two streams here flow out of the main river, driving a mill some little distance beyond, the lower stream being utilized and formed into a bathing place. Then comes the 'Gut', a curious bend in the river, often very disagreeable to racing eights, and a short mile below we reach Iffley.

---

* 'Friar Bacon's Study' was a tower with a gate and passage beneath which was supposed to date from the thirteenth century when it was built as a pharos or watch tower for the bridge. Tradition holds that it was used as a study by Roger Bacon, a Franciscan friar, with a reputation as an astronomer, and it was thought that if a greater scholar passed underneath 'it would undoubtedly fall'. It was removed in 1779.

The bridge at Nuneham Courtenay with a party of Thames visitors c. 1881

IFFLEY

IFFLEY LOCK from Oxford *1 mile 3 furlongs 150 yards; to Sandford, 1 mile 5 furlongs 70 yards: average summer fall, about 3 ft*

A boat slide close to the lock on the mill stream (*be cautious if the weir is running*) saves time for small boats.

Hotels – The 'Isis Tavern', above the Lock. The 'Tree', in the village, land above the Mill.

On the hill overlooking the river is the church, a splendid specimen of late Norman architecture, to which a visit can be paid before passing the lock. The church is finely preserved; its western façade, south door, and tower, are all in beautiful proportion, and richly carved with beak, zig-zag, and other ornamentation; in the interior the groining and arches being equally graceful, while a restored cross and fine old yew tree embellish the graveyard.

Just below the lock is the mill, once one of the prettiest on the river, but now shorn of its appendage of grand old trees.

Half a mile below comes the railway-bridge, over which the Thame and Wycombe Branch of the GWR passes, just above being the pumping station of the Oxford Sewage Works; the sewage, running to this place by gravitation, is forced up by the engine to the further side of the village of Littlemore, and there distributed on the farm.

Passing along a broad bit of stream – the scene in 1838, in 1855, and again in 1871, of sheep being roasted on the ice-covered river – we reach Rose or Kennington Island. Kennington village, on the other side of the railway, has one little inn, 'The Tandem', and a not very picturesque church. Beyond, on the rising ground, are the Bagley Woods, covering an enormous acreage, but closed to the general public.

ROSE ISLAND, KENNINGTON

Inn – 'The Swan'.

Station – Nearest railway station, Littlemore, GWR Thame branch; about a quarter of a mile.

A favourite place for dinner parties. Here the stream dividing bends suddenly round, joining again below the island, and a short distance beyond are Sandford pools. Beware of the side stream leading to them, unless you

River visitors at the lock cottages Nuneham Courtenay c. 1882

know it well, as the draught from the deep falling lasher is very great, and has been the cause of more than one disaster.

Sandford large pool is interesting from its grand splash of water, but dangerous for bathing, in consequence of eddies not quite understood. An obelisk, to the memory of two Christ Church men who were drowned, stands close to the main weir. The little weir pool opens straight out from the main stream, and must be avoided in high water time.

Fishing – The fishing for this distance below Oxford is not flourishing; partly owing, perhaps, to the immense boating traffic upon the river. The side streams are, of course, better than the main river, but are generally private water.

SANDFORD

SANDFORD LOCK from Iffley Lock *1 mile 5 furlongs 70 yards; to Nuneham, 2 miles 5 furlongs 160 yards: falls from 4 ft 6 in in high to 10 ft in low water; average in summer, about 7 ft 6 in*

Hotel – The 'King's Arms', close to the lock.

The mill, with its tall leaning chimney, is a notable object here. Sandford Church is partly Norman, but, after Iffley, is scarcely worth visiting.

A swift stream, below the lock, leads along Radley Common; in some places are shallows, which require a sharp look out from those in charge of steam launches and boats drawing much water. On the Oxfordshire side, the reedy flams harbour jack, chub, and other fish; and in some years gudgeons are plentiful, but in others none are to be found.

St Peter's College, Radley, standing on one of the old manors of the Abbey of Abingdon, about a mile across the fields from Sandford, is a well-known public school, whose increased reputation has raised it to a high place among the public schools of the country. The buildings, mostly of red brick, are picturesque; the interior of the chapel, with its richly-carved reredos and fine organ, very attractive.

Below Sandford we come to Nuneham, passing the mansion before we arrive at the picturesque cottages and bridge, just above which once existed a lock and weir.

SANDFORD LASHER & POOL.

SANDFORD MILL &c. *from below.*

AT NUNEHAM.

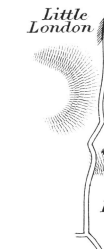

Little London

Radley College

Barn

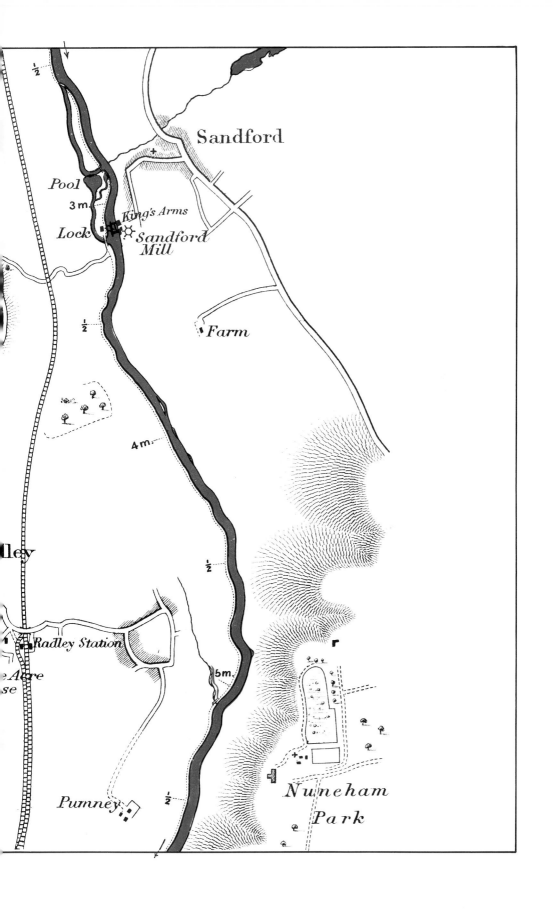

Sandford

Pool

3 m.

King's Arms

Lock

Sandford
Mill

½

Farm

4 m.

½

dley

½

Radley Station

Acre
se

5 m.

Pumney

½

Nuneham
Park

NUNEHAM

Nuneham Bridge – The middle arch of this bridge must be avoided, on account of the water way being blocked beneath it.

NUNEHAM from Sandford *2 miles 5 furlongs 160 yards; to Abingdon Lock, 1 mile 7 furlongs 60 yards*

The seat of the Harcourt family, and the favourite place for water parties from Oxford – is one of the prettiest spots on the river.

The park, which contains about 1,200 acres, extends along the Oxfordshire bank of the stream for nearly a mile and a half, and is beautifully varied by grand old trees and wooded glades rising from the river's brink. The prettiest part of the scenery is at the old lock, where the cottages and rustic bridge form, with the wood, a whole series of lovely pictures rivalling the most noted scenes on the river. Here it is that pleasure parties land; this being allowed on Tuesdays and Thursdays only during the season, by permission previously obtained from the agent, F. Mair, Esq.

On the hill, to which a pretty walk leads through the wood from the cottages, stands Carfax Conduit,* a picturesque arrangement in stone. It once stood on Carfax, Oxford, and then supplied water to the city, but was presented by the citizens to Simon, Earl Harcourt, who removed it to this spot. The conduit is a picturesque object in itself and worth a visit; from the hill are several extensive views, ranging up to Oxford and the hills beyond on the one hand, while, on the other, the spire of St Helen's, Abingdon, is seen, the view being bounded by the range of the Chilterns, finishing at White Horse Hill. From here to Clifton Hampden, across the park, is a distance of about two miles only, but the river makes a tremendous curve to get past the range of low hills on which we are standing, and makes the distance nearly four times as great.

* Carfax Conduit was built in 1610 by Otho Nicolson, treasurer to James I, to supply the city of Oxford with pure water. A most impressive and ornate design, it included statues of mermaids, dragons and unicorns, and Empress Maud riding an ox over a ford 'in allusion to the name of the city'. It was removed due to the widening of High Street and presented to Earl Harcourt.

Nuneham House is a little distance beyond the conduit, standing up on the hill from the river. It is in the Italian style, but owes its attractions to the beautiful gardens, which at one time were considered almost unrivalled. Amongst their best features at the present time are the rock grotto, the orangery, and rosary, with the western part of the terrace; while amongst minor beauties is the pleasant shaded walk leading to Whitehead's Oak,* where the combination of the old conduit with the foreground and distant foliage is very charming.

Station – Radley, GWR, Junction for Abingdon, about one and a half miles from Nuneham, on right bank.

ABINGDON LOCK from Nuneham *1 mile 7 furlongs 60 yards; to Abingdon Bridge, 3 furlongs 211 yards: falls from 5 ft in high to 7 ft in low water; average in summer about 6 ft*

The weir and overfall just by are picturesque, in spite of the new iron part of it, the drone of falling water being rarely absent, while Abingdon spire and bridge in the distance is very attractive.

Just below the weir is the bathing place belonging to the Abingdon Bathing Club (Secretary, Mr Leverett, Bath Street).

ABINGDON

ABINGDON BRIDGE from Oxford *8 miles 1 furlong 211 yards; to Culham Lock, 2 miles*

Abingdon Station (GWR branch), Stert Street, 2 furlongs from the bridge.

Abingdon is a very old town standing on the right bank of the river, which here is crossed by an ancient bridge built in 1416. Among its most noticeable features are the two churches, St Helen's, close to the river, built in the

---

* Whitehead's oak commemmorates William Whitehead (1715–85) who was appointed poet laureate in 1757. A friend of Earl Harcourt, he wrote various inscriptions on statues, tablets and urns which adorn Nuneham Park.

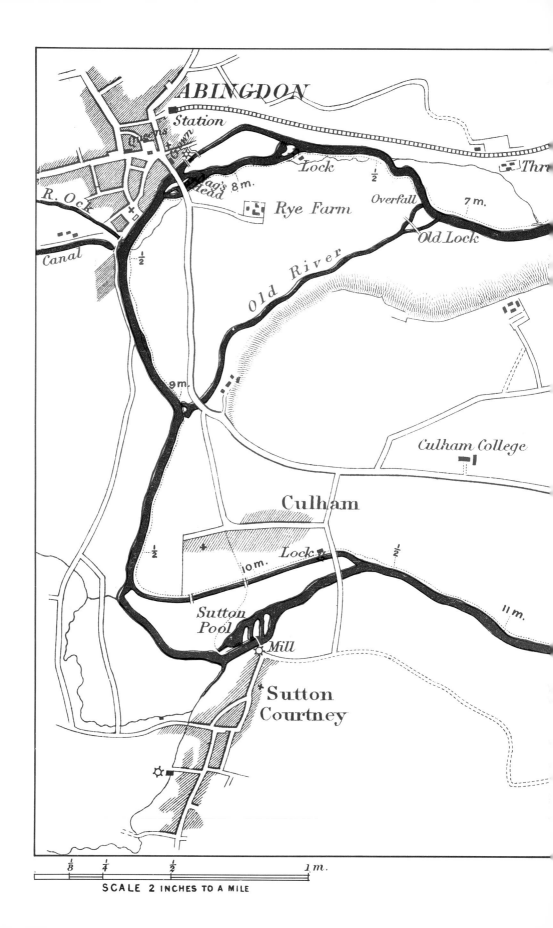

ABINGDON

Station

Lock
½

Thr

7 m.

R. Ock

Town

Ag's Head

8 m.

Rye Farm

Overfall

Old Lock

Canal

½

Old River

9 m.

Culham College

Culham

½

Lock

½

10 m.

Sutton Pool

11 m.

Mill

Sutton Courtney

⅛   ¼   ½   1 m.

SCALE 2 INCHES TO A MILE

Carfax

6 m.

Cottages

Wood

Nuneham *Park*

ABINGDON.

Clifton
Hampden

Plough

14 m.

Culham
Station

½

Barley Mow

Clifton
Farm

13 m.

Clifton
Lock

½

12 m.

Long
Wittenham

Appleford

A view of Abingdon above the bridge showing the premises of J. Stevens, boat builder and hirer c. 1899

fourteenth century, the spire of which is the first thing seen on approaching the town from the river, and St Nicholas', an old partly Norman edifice standing near the Market Place.

St Nicholas' Church, partly rebuilt about 1300 AD, has within the last few years been restored, the quaint features of its interior brought out, and an old inn (with its sign of the 'Two Brewers'), which obstructed the northern side, removed.

From the side of the church springs the gateway of the old Abbey, founded in Saxon times, and although ruined by the Danes, rebuilt and raised to great importance as one of the mitred Abbeys, the annual income when suppressed being equal to about £20,000 of present value. The only other remains of the abbey are the old mill, which still utilizes the waters of the side stream flowing from above the weir, a curious old chimney to be seen from the bridge among the houses on the Thames side near the mill, and a fireplace and vaults in the Abbey brewery.

On the side of the Abbey Gate stands the old Grammar School founded by John Royse, in 1568, now removed to a new building near the Albert Park.

In the centre of the Market Place, once stood the beautiful cross destroyed by Waller's soldiers in revenge for their defeat at Newbridge; the market house designed by Inigo Jones, forms one side of the square, while the new corn exchange and bank buildings lend dignity to the other.

St Helen's, restored 1885–6, is a magnificently large church, consisting of a spacious nave and chancel, with two aisles on each side; the eastern part of the north aisle forming a beautiful baptistry.

Close by, and forming the boundary to nearly three sides of the churchyard, are the almshouses; the western block, 'Christ's Hospital', is a picturesque building with quaint cloisters running along the whole front; the charter for which was granted by Edward VI in 1553.

Just outside the churchyard is Clarke, Sons, and Co.'s wholesale clothing factories, giving employment, indoors and out, to thousands of hands, and on the north of the town is a new pleasure park and recreation ground, with a handsome memorial to Albert the Good.

The Berks and Wilts Canal joins the Thames at Abingdon, the entrance lock being on the right bank, a short distance below St Helen's Church. It joins the Kennet and Avon Canal below Devizes, leading to Bath and the lower part of the Severn, and also by a branch on the right at Swindon, communicates with the Thames and Severn Canal near Cricklade, whence the Severn, the Warwickshire Avon, or the upper part of the Thames can be reached. The canal is in very poor order in places, but better below Swindon.

Boats Let or Housed – J. Stevens, just above the Bridge, also below St Helen's Church, landing place for hotels.

Hotels – The 'Queen's', in the Market Place; The 'Crown and Thistle', Bridge Street; The 'Nag's Head' (and landing place) on the bridge.

The Post Office is in the Market Place. It is open on weekdays from 7 a.m. till 10 p.m., and on Sundays from 7 a.m. till 10 a.m., and letters can be posted for London till 10 p.m.

Among the tradesmen we may mention Mr H. Hughes, for guide-books, views, and music; and Messrs Baylis and Co., for guides, views, and fancy goods.

Fishing – The fishing above Abingdon to Nuneham is good. Near Abingdon Bridge is a sharp stream, forming a fine scour for dace, etc.; and at Blake's pool are chub, barbel, etc. Above the lock the water is deep, and affords fine sport right up to the cottages at Nuneham for jack, perch, and chub, and above are several splendid swims.

Below Abingdon the water is not equally good, until we get to the reach by Culham Bridge, where jack are often very plentiful, and sometimes very large.

Fishermen – Walter Hyde, Charles Trinder, J. James.

Fish – Pike, tench, perch, dace, chub, barbel, etc. Bathing just below the weir, *see ante*.

A mile below Abingdon is Culham Bridge, an old structure of Henry VI's reign, and here the old navigation stream joins the river again, which spreads out into a bolder reach, from which the Culham Cut turns sharply out to the left, and leads past the little village of Culham to the lock; the main stream flows on to Sutton Pool and Mills.

CULHAM AND SUTTON COURTENAY

CULHAM LOCK from Abingdon Bridge *2 miles; to Clifton Lock, 2 miles 6 furlongs 130 yards: falls from 5 ft in high to 8 ft in low water; average summer fall about 7 ft*

This lock with Abingdon and Sandford make together a drop of over 20 ft in 7 miles, the greatest fall of the river within the same distance.

Railway Station – Culham (GWR), 1¼ miles from the lock.

Culham as a village has nothing of interest to note beyond the little church standing near the river. The Diocesan Training College stands by the side of the main road, half-a-mile from the bridge.

Sutton Pool (and weirs), a short distance across the fields to the right, has the reputation of being one of the deepest on the river. The weirs have been considerably enlarged in late years by the Conservators, who not only here, but in many other places have added to and augmented the waterway, so as to run off quickly the winter and summer floods. Iron in place of the old wooden weirs has been pressed into service, and although not picturesque like the old broken woodwork, yet has many advantages in other ways.

Sutton Courtenay is a picturesque village with a green in front of the church, and a road lined with trees leading from it. The church dates from Norman times; in the tower are round leaded windows of that period; the font is also of early date; but the interior sadly wants general restoration.

Below Culham the lock cut and stream again join, the latter being crossed by a well-built stone bridge of three principal arches, to cross over which a toll has to be paid; and from here a fine reach extends to Appleford Railway Bridge, abounding in jack and roach, though not much fished.

Appleford village is a short distance from the river, the church with its new white spire peeping from among the trees. In the distance is seen Sinodun Hill.

A mile below comes Wittenham Weir on the right bank round the sharp bend; and here the main river turns to the right, flowing by Long Wittenham village, the navigation being through the long cut to Clifton Lock.

CLIFTON

CLIFTON LOCK from Appleford Railway Bridge *1 mile 4 furlongs 54 yards; to Day's Lock, 2 miles 7 furlongs 180 yards: falls about 3 ft, varies but very little*

Half a mile below the lock is Clifton Bridge, a pretty newly-built structure crossing the river in the place of the old ferry, and just beyond is the picturesque little church, with its tasty spirelet finely situated on the top of a small gravel cliff shaded with trees, whose roots find sustenance in the clefts on the rock.

The church is worth the climb to see it. A beautiful edifice in the Decorated style of architecture; one of the best examples of the work of the late G.A. Street;* and its interior is equally good with the exterior.

---

* The restoration work of Clifton Hampden church was carried out by Sir George Gilbert Scott rather than by the late G. Street mentioned by Taunt.

Day's Lock with Wittenham Clumps in the distance c. 1904

The village also is very pretty, quaint old cottages peep out from amid the greenery, and the spirelet of the church overtops and makes a centre point in more than one lovely rural scene.

Railway Station – Culham (GWR), 1⅛ miles.

Inn – The 'Barley Mow' (land at the bridge house).

Fishermen – F. Casey, Butler.

Fish – Chub, jack, gudgeon, perch, eel, barbel, tench, roach.

Fishing – There is fairly good fishing all round Clifton. In the Wittenham Backwater are chub, jack, and barbel in large numbers; near Clifton Church are barbel* and roach, and below in many places are good pitches for a variety of fish.

The river makes a sharp curve here, and just below Clifton Bridge on the Berks side is extremely shallow. The deepest arch is that nearest the towing path; keep well round the curve with a boat drawing much water.

The hamlet of Burcott is the next place reached, but little of it is to be seen from the river, which bends round again to the south towards the foot of Wittenham Hills, but before we reach them Day's Lock has to be passed. The way to the lock is a cut to the left by the side of the island out of the main stream, the latter running straight to the new weir.

DAY'S LOCK

DAY'S LOCK from Clifton Bridge *2 miles 4 furlongs 40 yards; to mouth of River Thame, 6 furlongs 180 yards: falls from 1 ft in high to 5 ft in low water; average summer fall about 4 ft*

The scene at Day's Lock, with the flowing weir in the foreground, the old cottage and bridge beyond, and the background of hills, is very lovely, and this is only one of a whole series of pretty bits which abound on every hand. This place is a perfect mine for the artist, and a capital one too for the angler, as the pools are noted for their fine perch, and the reaches below and above for jack, perch, and chub.

There is also plenty of pleasure for the antiquarian in the surrounding

---

* 'I don't know if the barbel come to listen to the music in the church, or whether they are a religious fish', (says one of the fishermen), 'but they always get round the church, and more on Sunday than any other day in the week.'

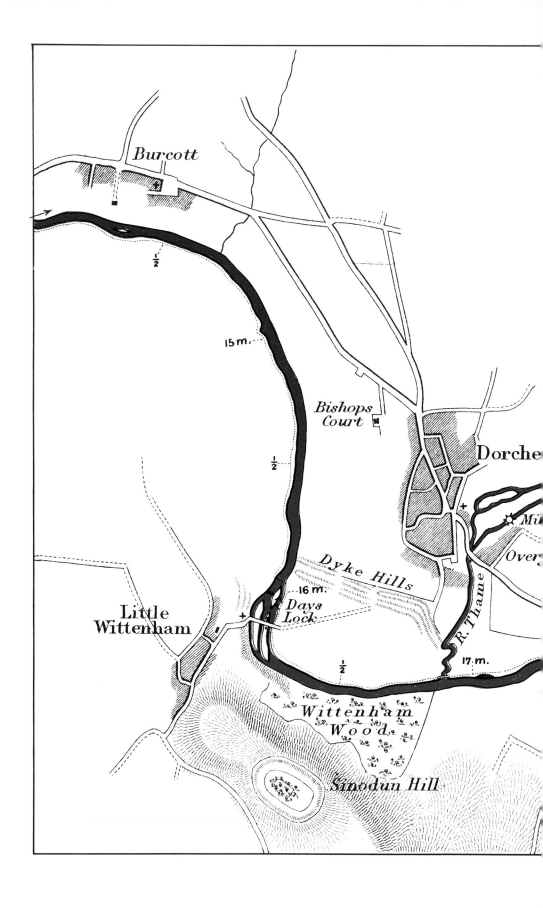

CLIFTON BRIDGE &c.

DAYS LOCK &c.

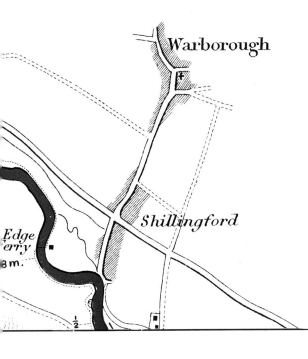

earthworks, and in the beautiful Dorchester Church, which lies only a short mile across the meadows.

A new weir replacing the old picturesque overfalls, etc., was completed in 1886. The lock being a little distance from the lock-house, a bell is placed with a wire hanging close above the top lock – right hand gate – to signal the lock-keeper; the call *below* is best given when passing under the iron footbridge crossing the river.

Three beds at the lock-house; and boats taken care of if required.

Bathing – From the island above the weir.

Wittenham hills are interesting from the remains of British or Roman camp fortifications which encircle the second hill (Sinodun), the fosse and ditch, with the various entrances, being still fairly perfect; and – if time – the toil of climbing will be amply repaid by the vast expanse of country seen from the summit.

Along the meadows between Day's Lock and Dorchester are a range of low mounds, the remains of British or Saxon earthworks; these have been partly levelled by the farmer who owned the land; but enough is still left to show the immense extent they cover, and create a wonder as to who were the people who carried out such a stupendous system of fortification.

A short mile below Day's Lock brings us to the mouth of the River Thame, which by some writers is supposed, by its junction with the Isis, to complete or make the River Thames; but a few yards up its waters will at once scatter any such theory to the winds, as it will be at once seen that the Thame is a mere rivulet compared with the volume of old Father Thames himself. This is the nearest point to visit

DORCHESTER

Dorchester stands on the River Thame. In the spring and early summer it may be possible to pull up to Dorchester Bridge, but in the autumn, if the weeds are grown, the wiser way will be to walk to the village and Abbey Church from the confluence of the river, more especially as you will on the way past through part of the earthworks we have before mentioned. Dorchester Abbey Church is one of the largest ecclesiastical edifices in the county, and has within the last few years, owing to the indomitable energy and private munificence of the late vicar, the Revd W.C. Macfarlane, been restored in a manner worthy of the magnificent building. The interior is equally beautiful with the outside, and contains among its other beauties, a grand imposing nave and chancel, with large side chapels. On the north side of the chancel the tracery of the window is formed into a tree springing from the loins of Jesse as he lies recumbent below, with carved figures on its trunk and branches, representing the genealogy of our Saviour, whose image crowns the whole.

Dorchester, in the time of the Saxons, was of great importance, it being a bishop's see, at that time the largest in England, and is stated to have contained other churches besides this grand old edifice. It has now dwindled into a large, quiet village.

Inns – The 'White Hart'; 'Fleur-de-lis'.

Fishermen – James Brown Turner; F. Batton.

Opposite the mouth of the Thame is Wittenham Wood, a favourite spot for picnics, where permission is freely given to camp, and from here the river flows tranquilly downward, passing Keen Edge Ferry on its way, and then with another turn or two reaches the village of Shillingford, which consists of a few houses only, some large malthouses, and a brewery, with an inn.

SHILLINGFORD BRIDGE

SHILLINGFORD BRIDGE from Day's Lock *2 miles 5 furlongs 200 yards; to Benson Lock, 1 mile 2 furlongs 30 yards*

At Shillingford Bridge the road from Oxford to Reading crosses the river, and, passing the hotel, winds along up the hill, from whence the best view is seen.

Hotel – The 'Swan'. Landing below the bridge.

Fishing – The fishing is very good, the water being preserved for a mile above and a mile below the bridge. Just above Shillingford village is a deep hole noted for its barbel, while every here and there the reedy flams furnish a splendid cover to the angler just where fish most abound.

SHILLINGFORD BRIDGE.

WALLINGFORD.

MONGEWELL CH.

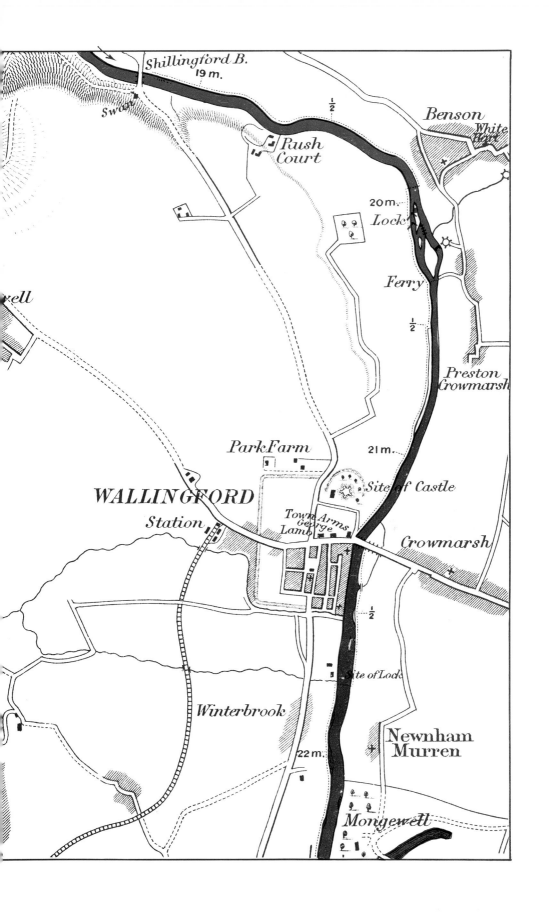

Wallingford Bridge and landing stage, and the Town Arm's Hotel c. 1892

BENSON (OR BENSINGTON) AND EWELME

BENSON LOCK from Shillingford Bridge *1 mile 2 furlongs 30 yards; to Wallingford Bridge, 1 mile 2 furlongs: falls from 3 ft 6 in in high to 6 ft 6 in in low water; average in summer, about 6 ft*

Be careful in high water time when going out or in at the bottom gate, as there is often a strong eddy from the weir, the rush of water over which is very wild and grand.

Omnibus – To Wallingford and back twice daily.

Benson was an important place in the old coaching days, when thirty or forty coaches passed through it each day..

Boats can be left at Benson wharf. A few yards below the wharf take the turn to the right to the lock, the main stream goes to the weir and mill. Benson wharf still retains a little of its river trade, which before the advent of railways was of vast extent: coal, timber, corn, and a variety of up-country produce being sent down from the west to London, Oxford, and other places, in barges and boats of large or small burden.

This is the nearest point to visit Ewelme, two miles to the left from the river (from Wallingford 3½ miles by road), a picturesque village, occupying one side of a little valley, with a beautiful church and almshouses. The church is Perpendicular in style, with large aisles on each side of the nave, the south chapel containing a magnificent altar, tomb, richly embellished with sculptured figures and shields and bearing the effigy of Alice, Duchess of Suffolk, the grand-daughter of the poet Chaucer. This monumental effigy has round its arm the Order of the Garter, being one of the three known examples of a lady wearing the order. There are tombs to the memory of Sir Thomas Chaucer and his wife, bearing richly quartered shields. The chancel screen also, and the exquisitely carved cover of the font are well worthy of notice.

Close to the church are the almshouses or hospital built by the Duchess of Suffolk, arranged round a beautiful cloister, which of itself would amply recompense for the visit any lover of architecture.

Hotels – The 'White Hart', The 'Crown'.

74

Fishing – In the weir pool are trout, perch, barbel, chub, and roach. Chub are to be found all along the tree-covered bank below Crowmarsh, and gudgeon often frequent the scours below the weirs in large numbers, while in the broad water above the lock are large pike and chub.

Fishermen – Frank Whiteman, Benson Lock.

Crowmarsh Ferry, with its pretty fringe of willow trees, is the next point to notice; not far below being Howbury Park, a large modern Elizabethan house, both on the left bank, while on the right, just before reaching the bridge are the mounds of earth, the site of the ancient stronghold, Wallingford Castle.

WALLINGFORD

WALLINGFORD BRIDGE from Oxford *21 miles 2 furlongs 91 yards; to Nuneham Ferry, 4 furlongs 70 yards*

Wallingford, like Oxford, is a very ancient town, being, it is said, the chief city of the Attrebatii* in Caesar's time. It was destroyed by the Danes in 1006, but soon rose from its ashes; and in the Domesday Book is said to have contained 276 houses. Wigod the Saxon (whose daughter married Robert D'Oyley, the founder of Oxford Castle) built a castle here, within which William the Conqueror, before proceeding to London after the battle of Hastings, received the homage of Stigand, Archbishop of Canterbury, and other of the chief men of Britain. The castle was strengthened after this, and encompassed by a double wall and ditch, and in Stephen's reign it received the Empress Matilda, who fled here for safety after escaping from the besieged Oxford Castle, by crossing the frozen river, the snow-covered ground and her white garments favouring her flight. Stephen followed her here, and blockaded the castle, erecting one at Crowmarsh on the opposite side of the river to keep it in check; and about this time, to save bloodshed, Stephen and Prince Henry met on an island in the Thames, and there it was arranged that Stephen should keep the crown for life, and be succeeded by Henry, who afterwards became Henry I. The mound of the keep is still visible above the bridge, and from here started the massive earthworks (to be seen at their best in the Kine Croft)

* An Iron Age tribe, of Belgic ancestry from Gaul, whose kingdom occupied Hampshire, Berkshire and parts of Sussex, Surrey and Wiltshire. It is now known that Silchester – *Calleva Atrebatum* in Hampshire – was the main settlement of this tribe.

The Old Lock House, Wallingford c. 1892

which encircled the town, and enabled the royalists to hold out for some time against Fairfax in the time of the Civil War. These, with the Market Square, containing an old-fashioned Town Hall, with St Mary's Church behind, the curious spire of St Peter's Church close to the bridge, said to have been designed by Judge Blackstone,* and the well-restored and beautiful little Church of St Leonard's (the interior of which, a fine specimen of late Norman, the chancel arch with its diaper ornamentation, being especially good and well preserved), a little farther down the river, are the lions of Wallingford. Crowmarsh Church, a couple of hundred yards on the opposite side of the river, is also Norman.

Station – (Branch Line, GWR), in the Wantage Road, about a quarter of a mile from the bridge.

Hotels – The 'Lamb', The 'George', The 'Town Arms'.

Boats Housed and to Let – Mrs Cloudesley, Town Landing, just above the bridge; W. Cope; J. Sparks, at the old lock house.

Fishing – At Wallingford Bridge and in the old lock pool are perch; below, in Mongewell Reach, chub and pike, a few barbel near the Wharf, gudgeon and dace along the scours in places, whilst at the flams, below Mongewell, are roach, chub, and jack.

Fishermen – W. Moody, E. Brant, F. Fleet.

The river below Wallingford Bridge has been dredged at an enormous cost by the Thames Conservators, and the flams and shallows cleared away. Wallingford Lock no longer exists. It was in an extremely dilapidated condition for some years; in the winter of 1881, the floating ice swept away the greater part of the weir, and at last the old lock, with the little island which formed its river side, was entirely removed.

This is now the longest reach between locks below Oxford, the distance from Benson to Cleeve being 6½ miles.

Bathing – At the Wallingford bathing place, close to the old lock.

A short distance below is Mongewell, a pretty park, with the white house and its diminutive church peeping out on the river, then a long flat reach with aits of rushes, and little to relieve the sameness of the landscape. The village of Mongewell has retained the same name ever since the Domesday Survey, when it belonged to Roger de Laci, and was worth £14. Close here is Grim's

---

* Sir William Blackstone (1723–80) was Recorder at Wallingford and first Professor of English Law. He was renowned for his *Commentaries on the Laws of England* written 1765–67.

MOULSFORD FERRY.

CLEVE LOCK.

STREATLEY.

Cholsey

G.W.R.

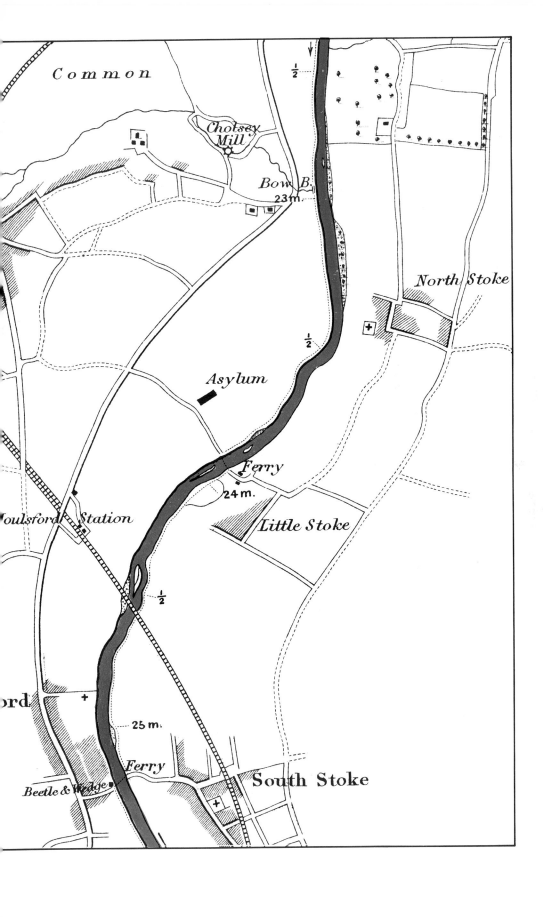

Cleeve Mill c. 1892

Dyke, or the Devil's Ditch, which consists of a vallum with embankment reaching some two miles or more across the country. North Stoke comes next, a little village, just as the corner towards Moulsford is reached, but a glimpse of its church tower is all which can be seen. The large brick building on the Wallingford side of the river is Moulsford Lunatic Asylum; the towing-path changes its side of the river at Little Stoke, and then comes Moulsford Railway Bridge, a path from the upper side of which leads to Moulsford Station (GWR, main line).

Fishermen – F. Strange, Bow Bridge.

Moulsford Railway Bridge is a splendid specimen of a skew bridge; and below the river broadens out into a wide and deep reach, which contains fine jack, chub, perch, and roach. These same fish are also among the aits and in the reach above the bridge, while below and near the Church are some capital perch, with gudgeon on the sandbank.

MOULSFORD

MOULSFORD FERRY from Wallingford, *3 miles 7 furlongs 180 yards; to Cleeve Lock, 1 mile 2 furlongs 78 yards*

Moulsford Church stands on the right bank of the river, and just below once existed an old mansion, the trees belonging to which form an extremely pretty bit, and a useful cover to a capital place for bathing in early morn. Next comes the picturesque Ferry, with its *Inn*, the 'Beetle and Wedge', where boats are to be let.

Below the ferry the broad open reach is a favourite sailing ground, but has been the scene of more than one unfortunate accident. At the lower end of the reach, on the left bank of the river, is a curious spring, the waters of which some few years ago were considered an infallible remedy for a variety of ailments, as well as sprains, bruises, etc.; close by the spring being the 'Leather Bottle' Inn. A bank, prettily shaded with trees, leads down the back water to 'The Temple' (a pretty ornate summer residence), and the Mill; but the navigation passes along the other side of the island, through Cleeve Lock.

Fishermen – A. Lovegrove, F. Cox (Moulsford), A. Garrett (Cleeve).

The Swan Hotel and landing stage, Streatley c. 1896

CLEEVE LOCK from Moulsford *1 mile 2 furlongs 78 yards; to Goring Lock, 5 furlongs: falls from 3 ft 6 in high to 5 ft in low water, average in summer, about 4 ft 6 in*

At Cleeve is the beginning of the lovely scenery that is to be found where the chalk hills of the Chiltern range approach the river; these now everywhere form the background to many artistic scenes, their beauty being augmented at Cleeve by the little islets and the pretty broken weirs and overfalls between them. Amongst these the most noticeable are the view from just above the lock looking towards Streatley, the overfall near the Mill, the Mill from below, and the view from Goring Field above the chalk pit, each of which exhibits a style of beauty entirely differing in character from the rest; and – besides these – lovely rural scenes abound all the way down to Streatley. This reach is the shortest between locks on the river, being only five-eighths of a mile, the next in length – that between Hurley and Temple – being 23 yards longer.

GORING AND STREATLEY

GORING LOCK from Cleeve Lock *5 furlongs; to Gate-Hampton Ferry, 1 mile 4 furlongs 127 yards: falls from 3 ft 6 in in high to 4 ft 6 in in low water; average in summer, about 4 ft*

Station – Goring (GWR, main line), 3 furlongs from the bridge.

Many travellers make a stop at Streatley or Goring, which are two of the prettiest twin villages on the river; and although the charm perhaps of the most romantic scenery is laid claim to by Streatley, still Goring has its beautiful old Norman church, and the great convenience of a railway station.

The country round Streatley is excessively lovely, the range of the Chilterns is to be seen here in all its beauty, and the health-giving walks up the hills, with their extensive and ever-varying scenery, make this one of the prettiest spots on the river. The village is a thoroughly rural one, not spoilt by the incursions of the multitude, and even the hotels, although now well supplying all wants, still bear evidence that they once were rural village stopping-places.

The scenery too amongst the aits and weirs, with the lock, and the two old mills, is very lovely; and the old wooden toll bridge which connects the two villages lends its charming picturesqueness in forming a series of beautiful pictures – so many and varied that there are few places more immortalised by artists than this. Streatley Church has been restored or rebuilt within the last

Streatley Mill c. 1896

few years; and although a good specimen of Early English style, has no special attractions. The old Roman way called the Icknield Street here crossed the river by a ford, and Streatley is stated to have derived its name from its situation on the old road.

At Aldworth, nearly three miles from Streatley, across the hills, is a Norman church, the interior of which contains a number of curious monumental effigies in stone, representing members of the family of De la Beche, who built a castle here, and were buried in the church. These figures, nine in number, received some injury during the Civil Wars at the hands of the Parliamentarians, but are still in tolerably good preservation. There is a quaint tale told by the old villagers respecting them.

Goring Church is an old Norman structure, its low tower pierced with two light windows, which from the bridge, in conjunction with the mill-stream, is most picturesque.

The interior is also worth visiting, the arcade with its massive chalk pillars and bold arches which unite the nave with the aisle, being worthy of note.

The following lines are an extract from *Punch*:

LAYS OF A LAZY MINSTREL
A Streatley Sonata

Ah! Here I am! I've drifted down –
The sun is hot, my face is brown –
Before the wind from Moulsford town,
   So pleasantly and fleetly!
I am not certain what's o'clock,
And so I won't go through the lock;
But wisely steer the *Shuttlecock*
   Beside the 'Swan' at Streatley!

But from the Hill, I understand
You gaze across rich pasture-land;
And fancy you see Oxford and
   P'raps Wallingford and Wheatley:
Upon the winding Thames you gaze,
And, though the view's beyond all praise,
I'd rather much sit here and laze
   Than scale the Hill at Streatley!

Camping out at Harts Wood c. 1880

And when you're here, I'm told that you
Should mount the Hill and see the view;
And gaze and wonder, if you'd do
    Its merits most completely:
The air is clear, the day is fine,
The prospect is, I know, divine –
But most distinctly I decline
    To climb the Hill at Streatley!

I sit and lounge here on the grass,
And watch the river traffic pass;
I note a dimpled, fair young lass,
    Who feathers low and neatly:
Her hands are brown, her eyes are grey,
And trim her nautical array –
Alas! she swiftly sculls away,
    And leaves the 'Swan' at Streatley!

Hotels – (Streatley) The 'Swan'; The 'Bull'. (Goring) The 'Miller of Mansfield'.
Boats Let or Housed – A. Saunders, Streatley; S.E. Saunders, Goring.
Fishing – The fishing at Streatley and Goring is thoroughly good: the waters being preserved for angling. In the weir pools splendid chub and other fish abound; whilst all up the river to Cleeve is excellent water, affording plenty of sport. Below, pike and perch are everywhere to be found, right down to Hart's Wood.
Fishermen – G. Bartholomew, J. Rush.
Fish – Pike, chub, perch, dace, roach, gudgeon, etc.

Below Goring the river winds along the foot of the hills for some distance, till it reaches the 'Grotto House', where the stream makes a bend and curves under the second brick viaduct of the GWR to the hills and woods on the other side of the river.

HARTS WOOD

Harts Wood is the vestige of one among those forests which centuries ago covered the whole of these hills, giving name to the Chiltern Hundreds, the

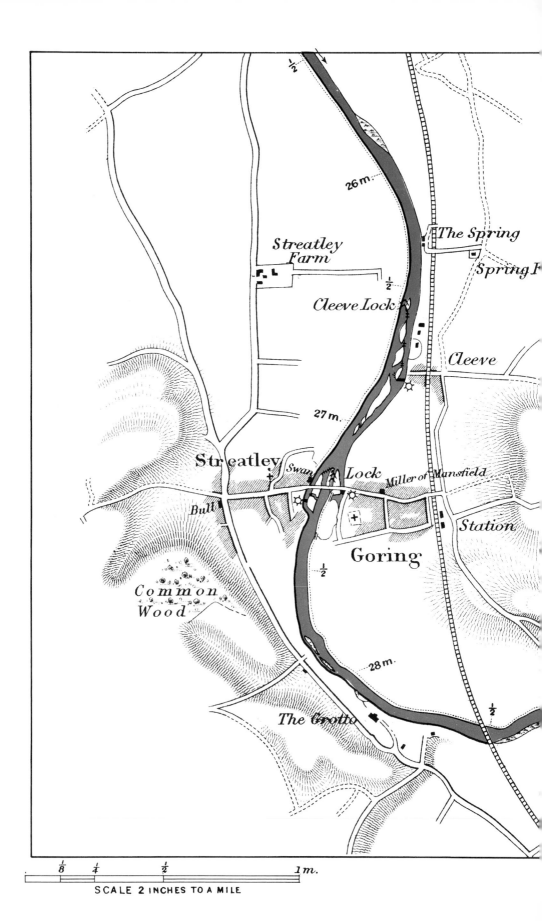

½

26 m.

The Spring

Streatley
Farm

Spring F

½

Cleeve Lock

Cleeve

27 m.

Streatley

Swan   Lock

Miller of Mansfield

Bull

Goring

Station

½

Common
Wood

28 m.

The Grotto

½

GORING CHURCH.

VIEW FROM GORING BRIDGE.

THE GROTTO.

29 m.

don

Harts Wood

The George Hotel landing stage, Pangbourne c. 1890

stewardship of which is usually accepted by a member of parliament when he wishes to vacate his seat. In those olden times, when the forests were infested with wolves, it was the duty of the stewards of the Chiltern Hundreds to protect travellers from their ravages: but of course the office is now a sinecure. These woods are very lovely; and the bit of greensward in front is a favourite camping-ground, permission being obtained from the owner at Coombe Lodge.

The flora of all these hills, around the woods and along the bank of the river, is very varied, and a bouquet of wild flowers can be culled here in the summer that will not be despised. Below, the river spreads itself out into a lake-like piece of water, which, bordered with beautiful trees on one side, and on the other stretching along the edge of Shooter's Hill, here rising nearly abruptly from the road and stream, on the right bank gives a capital opportunity for a series of lovely views. An old cottage once the 'Hole in the Wall', and another lower down lend animation and life to the scenery, whilst the rattle of the railway trains, hidden in the cutting through the hill, make music as they pass quickly along.

PANGBOURNE AND WHITCHURCH

WHITCHURCH LOCK from Basildon Ferry, *2 miles 4 furlongs 33 yards; to Mapledurham Lock, 2 miles 2 furlongs 70 yards: falls from about 3 ft in high to 4 ft 6 in in low water; average in summer, about 4 ft*

Station – Pangbourne (GWR), close to the river.
The way to the lock past the flowing weir in high water time requires a little caution, as the stream is strong, and it is wise on these occasions to hug the Oxon bank round the corner, until the lock is open for entering.

'Pangbourne is another of those pearls of English landscape which our river threads; no sweeter spot is within many miles. The Thames seems especially fond of disporting itself here; and loth indeed to leave, it loiters in the great depth of the pools, creeps slyly under the banks, frolics as a kitten after its tail in the eddies, and then dashes hurriedly off beneath the far-stretching, pretty wooden bridge, as if to make up for time truantly lost.'

The pool is a noted spot, not only for its beautiful bits, which are in endless

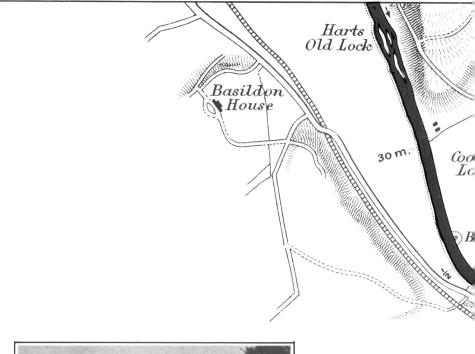

FROM SHOOTERS HILL.

FROM SHOOTERS HILL.

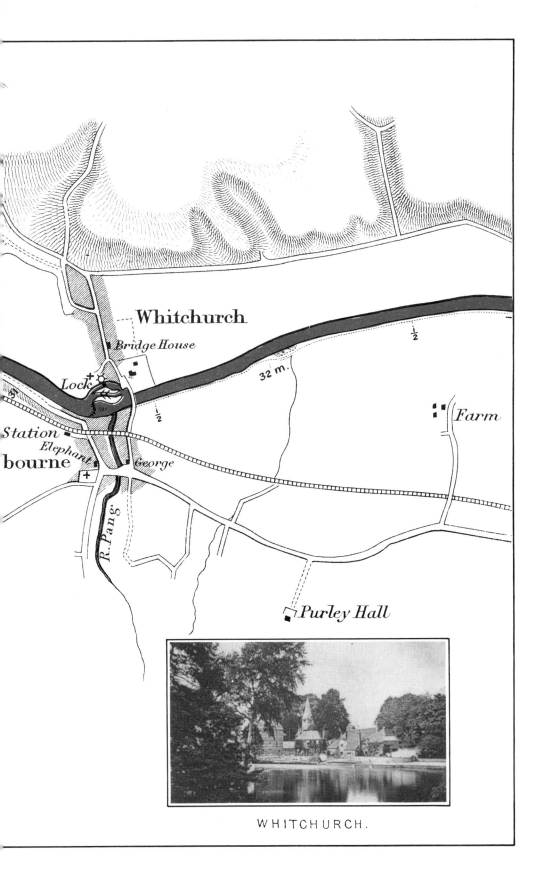

Whitchurch

Bridge House

Lock

$\frac{1}{2}$

32 m.

$\frac{1}{2}$

Farm

Station

Elephant

bourne

George

R. Pang.

Purley Hall

WHITCHURCH.

Pangbourne. The weir, and Whitchurch mill in the distance c. 1886

variety, but also for its fishing, the deeps of it being stated to harbour large fish; and in olden times it is said that as many as one hundred and fifty trout have been taken out in a single season. The Pang bourne runs into the Thames at this spot; it is renowned for its trout; but as far as fishing is concerned it is private property.

If stopping at Pangbourne, stroll through the wood-yard just below the weir, and note the extremely pretty grouping of the large ash trees with the different parts of the weir, and also with the bridge. From Whitchurch Bridge too, below the lock, the spire of Whitchurch and the mill-pool in combination make an effective landscape. Whitchurch Bridge is one of the few old-fashioned timber bridges on the river, which are fast passing away, being replaced by structures more adapted to modern times.

There are extremely pretty scenes all round Pangbourne, picturesque cottages and quaint bits are to be seen everywhere, beautiful walks are found in nearly every direction, up the valleys, through the woods, and over the hills, with great diversity of landscape; while the flora of the neighbourhood is more varied than in any other part of the Thames.

> Everywhere
> Nature is lovely . . . where around
> The undulating surface gently slopes
> With mingled hill and valley; everywhere
> The eye that seeks delight may find new charms.

Hotels – The 'George', land just above the Br; the 'Elephant and Castle'; the 'Swan'.

Coffee House and Reading-room – The 'Bear'.

Boats to be Let or Housed – E.T. Ashley, Pangbourne Wharf and above the weir. G. Ashley, the 'Swan', close to the weir.

Fishing – The fishing at Pangbourne is noted for its trout and jack, the weir pool being a favourite spot for these and other fish. Jack are in the deep water above the weir and in the reach below Whitchurch Bridge; perch and roach are also in large numbers along the edge of the reedy flams and the bank of the river towards Hardwicke House. The water is thoroughly preserved for angling.

Fishermen – G. Ashley, T. Lovegrove, Wm. Davidson.

Fish – Trout, perch, jack, barbel, chub, etc.

Bathing – in the weir pool.

Below Pangbourne the river is very pleasant, it stretches out into a broad

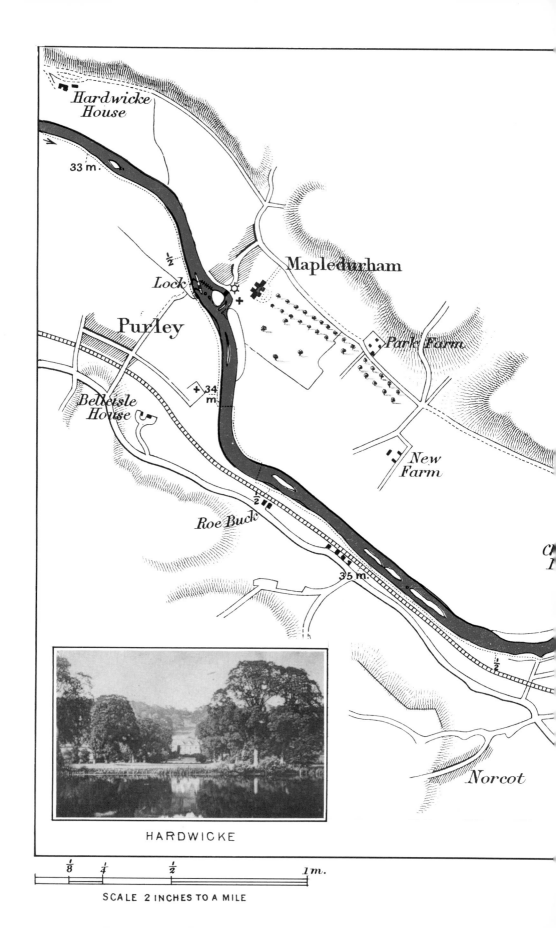

Hardwicke
House

33 m.

½

Lock

Purley

Mapledurham

Park Farm

+ 34
m.

Belleisle
House

New
Farm

Roe Buck

½

35 m.

½

CH
L

Norcot

HARDWICKE

⅛   ¼   ½   1 m.

SCALE 2 INCHES TO A MILE

MAPLEDURHAM.

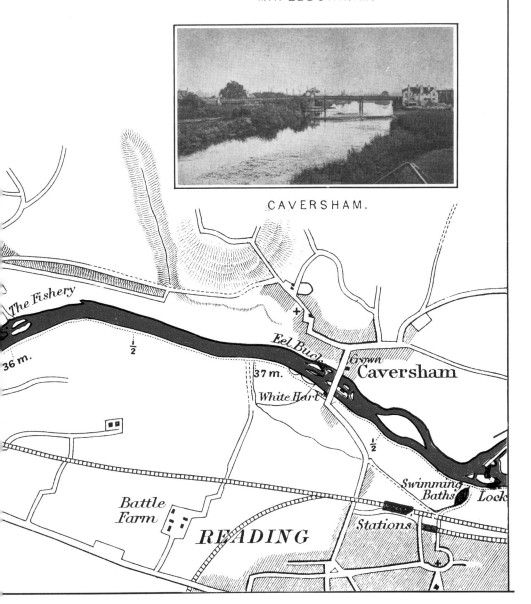

CAVERSHAM.

stream, partly filled with rushes and lined with trees; the hills approach nearer as Hardwicke House is reached, making a beautiful background to that charming old Tudor mansion, which is said to have been one of the hiding places for a time of Charles I.

Note also the scene up the river from just above the Lock with Hardwicke House for its centrepiece.

MAPLEDURHAM

MAPLEDURHAM LOCK from Whitchurch, *2 miles 2 furlongs 70 yards; to the 'Roebuck', 7 furlongs 145 yards: falls from 2 ft in high to 7 ft in low water; average in summer, about 5 ft 6 in*

About Mapledurham is one of the most lovely spots on the Thames. The view of the old Mill (the most picturesque on the river), with the combination of the church, peeping over its roof, and embosomed in foliage, forms one of the most tranquil scenes that it is possible to imagine, and needs nothing to add to its beauty and harmony; or seen from below, with the old water wheel throwing off its dripping spray in the bright sunshine and sending the foaming water rushing along from beneath, it presents an equally lovely, though entirely different, picture.

The church stands below the Mill, between it and the Manor House. It is in a beautiful situation, surrounded with trees, and was restored in 1864. The south aisle is the ancestral burial place of the Blounts.

The Manor House of Mapledurham is a splendid specimen of the Elizabethan style; indeed there are few in any part of England that are finer or in better preservation. It has always belonged to the family of the Blounts, and is still in their possession. From the front of the house there extends a broad avenue of elm trees, about a mile in length, forming a magnificent setting to a noble picture.

The house was garrisoned for the king, by Sir Charles Blount, in the time of the Civil Wars. The poet Pope used to visit Mapledurham House, when paying his addresses to Miss Blount, to whom some of his most charming letters were addressed.

Mapledurham Lock is, in its combination with the weir, one of the prettiest locks on the Thames; and the weir being always overflowing adds to the charm by its rolling melody, which varies in degree as the wind blows or moderates the sound. Mapledurham is essentially a 'painter's paradise'.

No inns at Mapledurham.

Fishing – The fishing here is known for its large trout, jack, chub, and perch. The water is preserved for angling throughout the district, beginning where the Pangbourne preservation water ends, and below joining that of the Reading Society.

Fisherman – Edward Shepheard (Purley).

A swift stream for a little distance leads past the island below Mapledurham, then amongst the grand old planes and elms on the right bank is seen Purley Church, isolated, and standing apart with its accompaniment of tombstones only.

At the curve of the river the Great Western line again runs parallel with the stream, its rattling burden of heavy trains passing so often at times seem quite continuous; a little lower is the 'Roebuck' Hotel, perched up aloft on a high bank over the railway; and below the new Tilehurst Station on the same line; whilst looking back Purley House is to be seen amongst the trees.

Hotel – The 'Roebuck'.

The river below is broken up by islands, but can scarcely be termed picturesque, the banks, particularly on the railway side, being quite uninteresting. At thirty-six miles from Oxford are some Eel Bucks, the stakes of which must be avoided by keeping well to the towing-path side of the high post, just before reaching which is a sharp series of eddies which, in high water time, are rather inconvenient, although not dangerous. This used to be a very fair bathing-place, but the Conservancy have stopped the bathing by ballasting some frightful holes, and these are partly the cause of the eddies. From this place to Caversham there is no point of interest, the river banks being flat and unattractive. At Caversham a number of new villa residences are springing up at Caversham Hill, along the pretty Mapledurham road; and the church tower peeps over the trees as we near the bridge.

Fishing – The river from the 'Roebuck' is well stocked with jack, perch, and chub. Barbel are to be found at the scours and in Caversham Pool, and gudgeon from Mapledurham Lock all along the scours in large numbers. Jack are nearly everywhere from Tilehurst Station to Caversham Lock, and more especially in the broad near the Fishery and round the Caversham Islands. Trout are fairly plentiful, and will no doubt largely increase, as the Reading Angling Associations stock the river with a large number every year, averaging in weight from 1 to 3 lb.

Caversham Bridge, with E. Causton's boat building establishment on 'Centre' or Piper's Island c. 1895

CAVERSHAM

CAVERSHAM BRIDGE from Mapledurham Lock, *3 miles 6 furlongs 131 yards; to Caversham Lock, 4 furlongs 120 yards*

This plain iron structure stands on the site of an old brick bridge, whose roadway was so narrow that two vehicles could not pass upon it and the arches were small and many in number. It witnessed a repulse of the fiery Prince Rupert and his cavaliers who attempted to raise the siege of Reading, but the narrow barricaded bridge effectually prevented their assistance being given to the beleaguered town.

Caversham Church has lately been nearly rebuilt, and, with its western tower, forms a pretty centrepiece in the scene from the bridge.

Just below Caversham Bridge is the large island on which the gage of battle was fought between Robert de Montfort and the Earl of Essex, in the presence of Henry II; the latter who was accused of cowardice, being defeated; but was allowed to save his life by becoming a monk of Reading Abbey.

Hotel – 'Caversham' Hotel.

Boats Let and Housed – W. Moss, Oxon shore, E. Causton, Centre Island, T. Freebody, Oxon Shore, A.D. Bona, 'Caversham' Hotel.

Fishermen – W. Moss, H. Knight, G. Knight, H. Rush, W. Clark.

Buses run to Reading and back about every half-hour.

READING

Railway Stations – All close together, about half a mile from Caversham Bridge; about 3 furlongs from Caversham Lock.

GWR, main line. This station is divided into two distinct parts, the up station being the new building facing the entrance from Friars Street, and the down station the old one further below, from whence also the trains start for the branch lines to Newbury, Hungerford, Basingstoke, etc. SWR, Reading branch, to Staines and London; SER, Reading branch (both run into same station).

Reading, the county town of Berkshire, is situated on the River Kennet, which, passing through its centre, enters the Thames at Kennet's Mouth. It is a growing market town, and contains some famous manufactories and other branches of commerce, amongst which are the Biscuit Factory of Messrs Huntley and Palmers, giving employ to some 3,500 hands, and the immense Seed Warehouses of Messrs Sutton and Sons in the Market Place, in connection with their acres of gardens. These can both be visited by order obtained on application.

Its greatest attractions are the remains of its once celebrated Abbey, the ruins of which are carefully preserved, and – with the Forbury – formed into beautiful pleasure gardens, open and free to the public. The Abbey was founded by Henry I, and endowed in the most princely manner, the abbot being a baron, with a seat in Parliament, and privileges wider than was usual even with Lord Abbots. The body of Henry (who died at Rouen, in France) was embalmed, wrapped in bull hides, and brought to Reading, and buried with great pomp in this Abbey he had founded. In 1539 the Abbey was dissolved by Henry VIII, the last abbot with two priests being hung, drawn, and quartered, for denying the King's supremacy.

In 1643 Reading was besieged by the Parliamentarian troops under Essex, and although a brave stand was made, it was forced to surrender, the attempt to raise the siege being unsuccessful. The Abbey suffered very much during and after the siege, and since then was looked upon as a quarry, the whole of the facing stone being removed for other buildings, and only the inner rubble of the walls left. The gateway has been restored, and is used as the armoury for the volunteers. Of the remains of the Abbey perhaps that of the Hall is the most striking; here the rubble walls show plainly the grandeur of its form and size; other large ruins are clustered round it, and from one point a curious formation of the 'Queen's head' is made by the combination of some of the broken walls seen through an opening in them.

The Abbey ruins are often utilized for fêtes, flower shows, etc.; they form a charming resting-place if a little time to spare in Reading.

The churches in Reading are not without attraction. That of St Lawrence in the Market Place, and St Mary in the Butts, are beautiful specimens of flint and stone churches, each with a square western tower. St Giles's has a tall spire, which has been rebuilt, and several churches, amongst them the beautiful Christ Church, have been added within the last few years.

New municipal buildings also have lately been erected, the expense being partly raised by subscriptions; but the architecture is not so pleasing as might have been anticipated from the cost with the exception of the entrance tower, which also boasts a set of carillons.

The chief Post Office is in Broad Street, and open on week days from 7 a.m.

till 9 p.m., on Sundays from 7 a.m. till 10 a.m. the last post leaving for London at 2 a.m. There is also a letter-box near Caversham Bridge.

Hotels – The 'Great Western', close to railways, The 'Vastern', close to the stations, The 'Beehive', Commercial, Friars Street, The 'Queen's', 'Wheatsheaf', Friars Street.

Among the principal trades we notice Messrs Sutton & Sons the well-known Queen's Seedsmen, in the Market Place. Lovejoy's Old Established Library, etc. (Proprietor E. Langley), in London Street. Mr Beecroft's in the Market Place, for Views, Stationery, and Printing. Messrs E. & J. Blackwell, for Printing, Stationery, and Views – also in the Market Place; and Messrs Turner Brothers, Duke Street, for Guides, Views, Printing Stationery, etc.

Bathing – the Reading Bathing Pool, just above Caversham Lock.

CAVERSHAM LOCK from Oxford *37 miles 7 furlongs 170 yards; to Sonning Lock, 2 miles 4 furlongs 148 yards: falls from 1 ft in high to 4 ft in low water; average in summer, about 3 ft 6 in*

Be careful in high water to hug the towing-path shore when entering from above, as the draught from the weir is very strong.

Caversham Weir was rebuilt in 1884, an iron weir being substituted for the old picturesque Clappers. A path over the lock gates and a footbridge, crossing the weir, leads to Lower Caversham and the Mill. There is a good swinging stream past the Reading Recreation Ground and the Mill, over the 5 furlongs 120 yards between here and Kennet's Mouth, where the River Kennet joins the Thames. This river is made navigable to Newbury; and there, being connected with the Kennet and Avon Canal, forms a complete navigation to Bristol and the West of England.

Boats to be Let and Housed – Arthur East.

Fishing – From Caversham Lock to Sonning are roach and jack in plenty. Chub lie under the willows, with dace on the scours at Caversham Hill and Sonning Oaks. In the Kennet, near the pumping station, are barbel and trout, often of a good size, whilst above, in the pool of County lock, are also trout and barbel. The largest trout ever taken from the river was captured here by a Reading fisherman, and presented to the Queen. It weighed nearly 17 lb. A capital cast was taken of the fish, and is preserved in the smoking-room of the Great Western Hotel.

After receiving the water of the Kennet, the Thames runs for some distance

Sonning Bridge and the White Hart Hotel and landing stage 'for launches of any draught'

c. 1900

through a belt of flat meadows, with willow trees on the left bank, through which is to be seen in the distance Caversham House, where Charles I was kept a prisoner for some time; then making a sudden bend past some islands covered with foliage, it sweeps round to the hills and woods of Holme Park, at the edge of which is a very pretty walk along the river's side beautifully shaded by the overhanging trees. A short distance along this lovely Thames parade brings us to Sonning Lock.

SONNING

SONNING LOCK from Caversham Lock, *2 miles 4 furlongs 148 yards; to Shiplack Lock, 2 miles 6 furlongs 126 yards: falls from 2 ft in high to 5 ft in low water; average in summer, about 4 ft*

Nearest Station – Twyford (GWR), from Sonning, 2 miles.
A 'bus leaves Sonning for Reading every day at 11.30 a.m. and 6 p.m., and Reading for Sonning at 9 a.m. and 4 p.m. On Sundays, from Reading at 6 p.m., from Sonning at 8 p.m. Fare 6*d*.

The river at Sonning is very pretty, and is broken up into a number of streams with islands between, on which in May the snowflake grows, and with its pale cold flower tells of the coming summer.*

At the lock are Sadler's bees, kept by the lock-keeper, the son of the well-known old man who had charge here for so many years, but who has gone to his well-earned rest.

The church stands close to the river, and is mostly in the Early Decorated style of architecture, the graveyard being well kept and very tasteful. The interior contains amongst other architectural beauties a chancel arch adorned with sculptured figures. Lately, a beautiful reredos has been added, and a tomb to the late rector.

The view of the bridge below, in combination with the church, is one of the favourite bits of artists; and in old times, when Sonning was the seat of a bishop, it was no doubt of more importance, but could not at any time have been a pleasanter resting-place than at present.

---

* The snowflake or leucojum is a bulb with flowers resembling the snowdrop, though more rounded in appearance. The 'summer snowflake' species flowers in April and May.

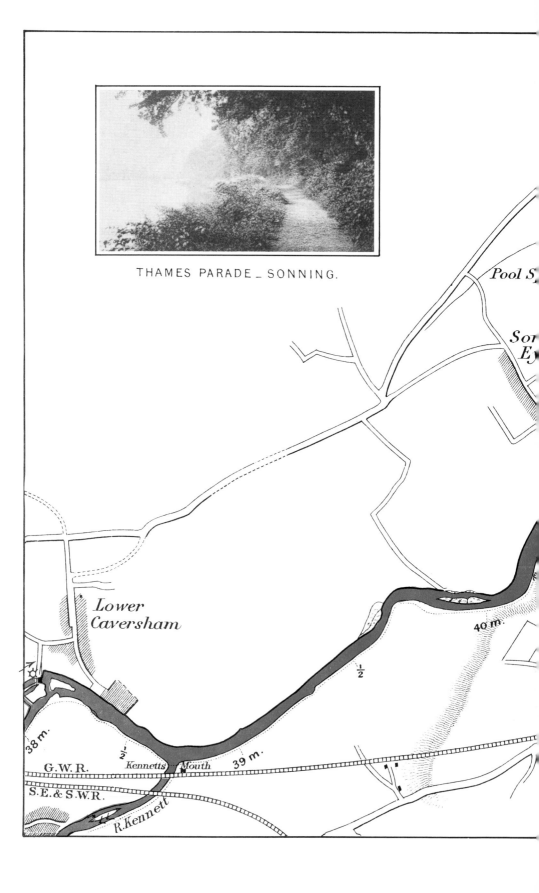

THAMES PARADE – SONNING.

Pool S

Sor
E

Lower
Caversham

40 m.

½

38 m.

½

39 m.

G.W.R.   Kennetts Mouth

S.E. & S.W.R.

R. Kennett

Shiplake

Burrow Farm

½

42 m.

½

41 m.

Sonning

White Hart

Hundred Acres

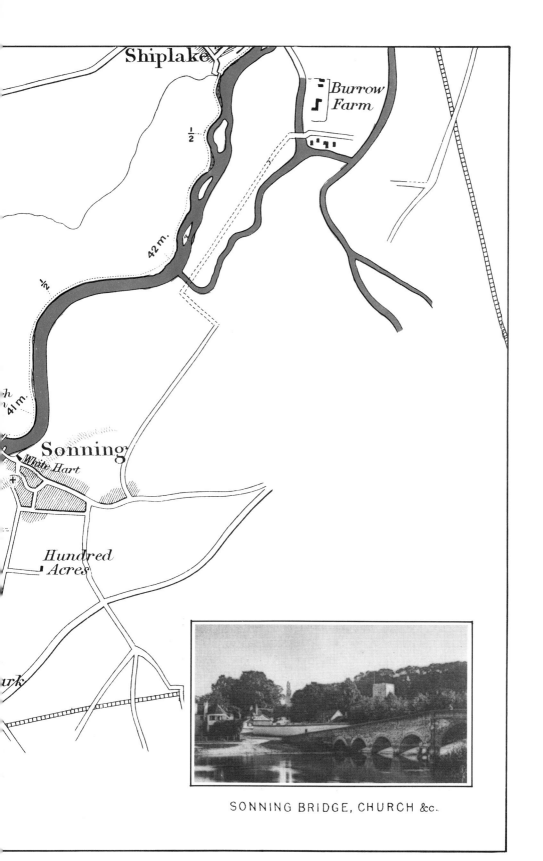

SONNING BRIDGE, CHURCH &c.

View near Shiplake weir with anglers c. 1900

THE FRENCH HORN,

SONNING, near READING.

Very pleasantly situated on the banks of the Thames.

FRENCH HORN HOTEL, SONNING.

It has been entirely Rebuilt and Refitted, with all modern improvements and comforts, and affords the best of accommodation, making up nearly 40 beds.

BOWLING GREEN AND TENNIS COURT.

FRENCH HORN, SONNING.
W. HULL, Proprietor.

A watercart beside the Thames at Shiplake c. 1875

Hotels – The 'French Horn', on the backwater stream, under the towing-path bridge. The 'Bull', through the churchyard, the 'White Hart'.
Boats Let and Housed – T. Sadler, at the Lock.
Fishing – The fishing at Sonning is very good. The lock-pools are the private property of Mr Witherington, and part of the backwater is rented by W. Hull, at the 'French Horn'. Permission to fish is freely given by Mr Witherington (except when previously engaged).
Fishermen – H. Rush (Reading), W. Clark.
Fish – Trout, barbel, chub, jack, perch, roach, dace, etc.
Bathing – Close above the lock, in the back stream from the island; bathing house and camping ground close by.

The river below Sonning loses all its beauty for a short distance, till near Shiplake, where islands again divide the stream, and the church perched on the hill behind the chalk pit varies the landscape. A side stream turns out here to join the Loddon, which runs again into the Thames below Shiplake Lock, and forms a curious link between the two rivers; just by its exit being a favourite artistic group of eel bucks behind the island.

Shiplake Weir comes next; it has been rebuilt about 200 yards below the old one, in a more convenient place, and the water-way enlarged; so that in high water care must be taken not to get too near, as the draught from the fall is considerably greater than it used to be.

SHIPLAKE LOCK from Sonning Bridge, *2 miles 4 furlongs 66 yards; to Shiplake Ferry, 1 mile 0 furlongs 38 yards; falls from 1 ft 6 in in high to 4 ft in low water; average in summer, 3 ft 6 in*

Shiplake Lock, with the picturesque mill close by, has all the makings of a picture in its composition, and has more than once been transferred to a canvas which has graced the walls of the Academy. Just below where the weir stream joins, the Thames receives the waters of:

The Loddon slow, with silver alders crown'd

which, rising near Basingstoke in Hampshire, passes Strathfieldsaye, the seat of the Duke of Wellington, and then along the borders of Windsor Forest, past Twyford into the Thames.

This stream is immortalised by Pope in the fabled story of Lodona in his poem of 'Windsor Forest'.

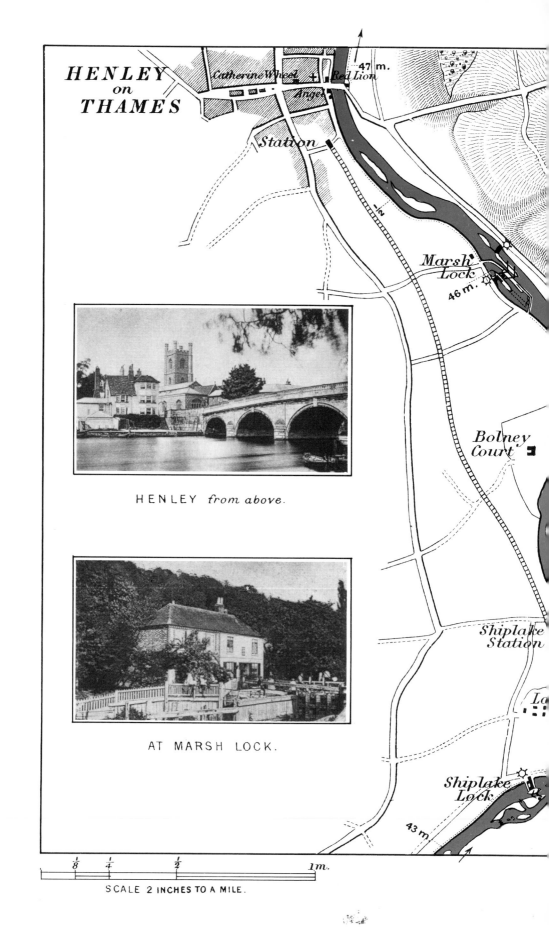

HENLEY on THAMES

Catherine Wheel
Red Lion
Angel

47 m.

Station

Marsh Lock

46 m.

Bolney Court

Shiplake Station

Shiplake Lock

43 m.

HENLEY *from above.*

AT MARSH LOCK.

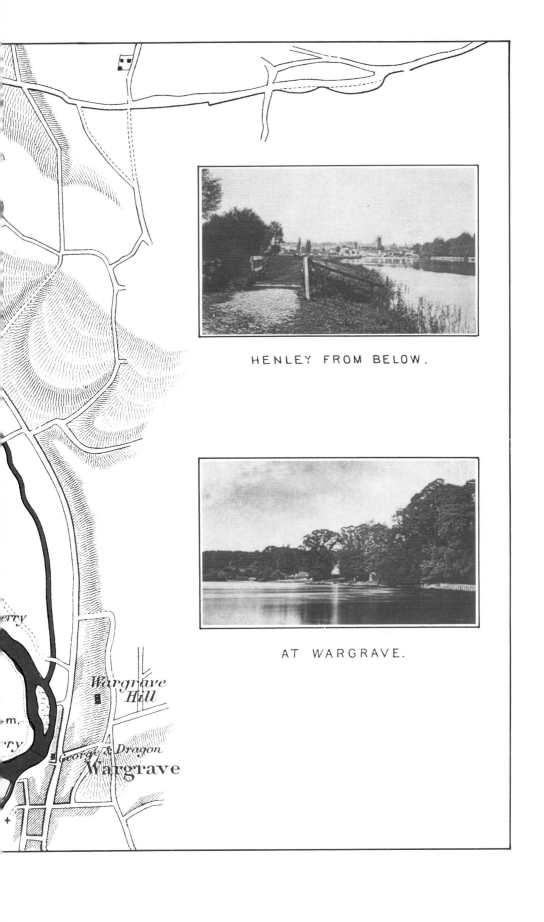

HENLEY FROM BELOW.

AT WARGRAVE.

A backwater of the Thames at Wargrave c. 1890

Bathing and camping ground at the lock by arrangement with the lock-keeper, who has also a lock-up bungalow with beds.

After passing under the railway bridge, over which run the branch trains to Henley, we soon arrive at the village of Wargrave.

WARGRAVE

Very pleasantly shaded by stately trees, Wargrave was once a market town, but has been left behind in the race of life, and gradually subsided into a quiet country village. And a pleasant village it is, with its one street leading down to the church, which is a fine well-restored building, in several styles of architecture; and contains, among other interesting objects, a monumental tablet to the memory of the author of *Sandford and Merton*, Mr Day, who was killed here by a fall from his horse.* Wargrave has generally a resident artist or two, and the sign of the 'George and Dragon', the hotel at the ferry, bears evidence of their work. 'St George' is represented on one side of the sign at his orthodox employment of killing the Dragon; whilst on the other – by a freak of fancy – he is tossing down the beer from a tankard, in the way a thirsty Englishman often does after a spell of excessively hard work.

Nearest Railway Station – Shiplake (GWR, Henley branch), 6 furlongs from the Ferry.

Hotels – 'George and Dragon', 'White Hart', 'Bull'.

Boats Housed and Let – E. Wyatt & Sons, at the Ferry.

Fishing – From Shiplake to Marsh Lock. Roach, gudgeon, and perch abound, and in some of the backwaters are fine pike. Shiplake-pool is noted for its trout and pike; Marsh-pool for its barbel; and all the way down are fine scours and deeps affording good fishing right to Henley.

Fishermen – S. Crampton, F. Wyatt, W. Brown, H. King, W. Ellsley.

Fish – Jack, chub, perch, tench, roach, dace, gudgeon.

Bathing – the lock-pool; also behind the island just below Wargrave in early morning.

---

* Thomas Day (1748–89) was greatly interested in educational theory and natural upbringing. His celebrated children's book *The History of Sandford and Merton* in three volumes, 1793–99, was very popular and was translated into several languages. He was killed when he fell from his horse while journeying from his home near Chertsey to his mother's residence at Bear's Hill near Wargrave.

W. REDKNAP, Queen's Waterman, by Appointment.

MEAKES & REDKNAP,
ENGINEERS,
STEAM LAUNCH AND BOAT BUILDERS,
BRIDGE WORKS AND VICTORIA BOAT HOUSES
(ABOVE BRIDGE),
GREAT MARLOW.

STEAM LAUNCHES (ALL SIZES), HOUSE BOATS, ROWING BOATS,
PUNTS, CANOES, ETC., OF EVERY DESCRIPTION,
LET ON HIRE BY THE HOUR, DAY, WEEK, MONTH, OR SEASON.

**Gentlemen's Boats attended to, Housed, Repaired, and
Varnished.**

*DRESSING ROOMS, LAVATORIES, AND EVERY CONVENIENCE FOR LADIES
AND GENTLEMEN BOATING.*

Steam Launches taken out of the water on Improved Slip-ways, for
Repairs, or Housed for the Winter.

*Repairs, Alterations, and Additions of all kinds undertaken; also
Painting and Varnishing.*

STEAM-LAUNCH REQUISITES KEPT.

*The British Pure Ice Company's Ice can always be had at the Boat Houses, in small
or large quantities, at Reasonable Prices.*

Pending the completion of our Works and Boat Houses we have
taken the River Frontage of the "Anglers" Hotel, where Boats of all
kinds will be taken in and Let throughout the season.

The great advantage of both our Boat House and "Anglers" Hotel
Frontages is, they are on the private side of the river, so that our
patrons will be saved the annoyance of the public towing-path.

*P.S.—A Boat always in readiness to fetch Ladies and Gentlemen across from the.
Towing-path opposite our Boat Houses.*

Telegrams :—MEAKES REDKNAP, MARLOW.

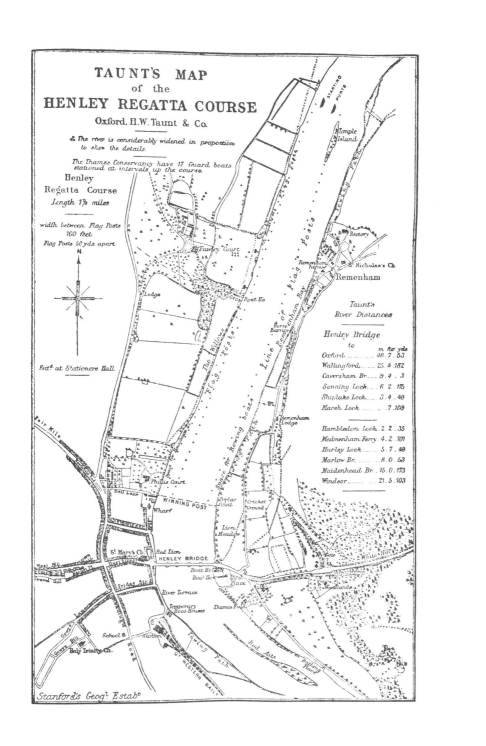

Henley Regatta. 'Steward's Cup, 2nd Heat New College and London final' c. 1895

A short distance below is Shiplake Ferry, and on the left bank of the river, a little farther on, Shiplake Railway Station; then nothing of interest till Boulney Court, a stone-built house, remarkable at first sight for the immense number of chimneys it seems to possess.

Next follow the grounds of Park Place, the river expanding into a lake-like piece of water, with towering white cliffs extending along the right bank, and a little plot of greensward betwixt them and the stream. A little farther on is a peep through an arch built of the facing stones from Reading Abbey, and then a very pretty Gothic boat-house looks down upon the river.

Besides the house, the Druid's Temple,* presented by the inhabitants of Jersey to the late General Conway, the then owner of Park Place, is one of the objects of interest; and permission to view these magnificent grounds can generally be obtained by sending a previous request. The Wargrave road to Henley winds along the top of the cliffs, over the Park Place Bridge; and several pretty peeps are to be seen from it. The towing-path passes over a long wooden pile bridge, by the head water of the new weir, and in the centre of it is Marsh Lock.

MARSH LOCK from Shiplake Ferry *2 miles 0 furlong 82 yards; to Henley Bridge, 7 furlongs 109 yards: falls from 2 ft in high to 4 ft 6 in in low water; average in summer, about 4 ft*

At Marsh Lock is the first view, in the distance, of Henley; the stream being fairly fast over the short mile which intervenes. Before reaching it, note the Henley Bathing Company's Establishment at Solomon's Hatch, behind the islands, and the beautiful rolling slopes of Park Place filling up the background.

---

* The 'Druid's Temple' was discovered on a hilltop near St Helier in Jersey in 1785. Recognized as a megalithic tomb, it was required to be removed from its original site and was given to General Conway, when retiring from his post as Governor of Jersey, due to his interest in the monument. Hence it was set up in the grounds of his house, Park Place, on the Thames.

HENLEY

HENLEY BRIDGE from Oxford *46 miles 7 furlongs 53 yards; to Putney Bridge, 57 miles 4 furlongs 13 yards*

Henley Station – (GWR, branch), 2 furlongs from the Bridge.

Henley, according to Dr Plot,* is the oldest town in Oxfordshire, but exhibits few traces of great age. Its charm consists chiefly in the beautiful reach of the river, which makes it beyond all others the grand meeting place of the amateur oarsman on the occasion of the Regatta, which annually takes place here. The bridge, a fine stone structure of five arches, has its centre keystones ornamented by the chisel of the Hon Mrs Damar,† with allegorical representations of Thames and Isis, the former on the lower side of the bridge, representing a bold classical head, with fishes swimming from between the flowing beard, and the latter, on the upper side, exhibiting a beautiful female head, the ideal of the goddess Isis.

The church, a fine Late Decorated edifice, stands close to the bridge, its bold turreted tower forming a steering guide up the course. The architect is said to have been Cardinal Wolsey. Henley is not a large town, but its principal street is not without some beauty; and the entrance to the town along the Oxford Road, called the 'Fair Mile', is one of the noblest in England.

Henley Amateur Regatta is the largest and most important of the English regattas: it is visited by the *élite* of the aquatic world, and during its continuance the town is the centre of a very fashionable gathering.

The Regatta had its origin in a contest between the Universities of Oxford and Cambridge in 1829, which led to the idea of its becoming annual, and the difficulties being overcome, it was fairly started in 1839, and has grown to its present extensive dimensions.

---

* Dr Robert Plot (1640–96), the Oxfordshire historian, famous for his *Natural History of Oxfordshire* written in 1677. He was also Secretary to the Royal Society and first Keeper of the Ashmolean Museum.

† The Hon Mrs Damar (1748–1828) was the daughter of General Conway of Park Place, Henley. A lover and connoisseur of art, she was a famous sculptress. Her cousin, Horace Walpole, left her his gothic mansion 'Strawberry Hill' for her use during her lifetime.

The new course, altered in 1886, is the centre of the splendid reach of river from about a hundred yards below Temple or Regatta Island to near the bridge, a distance of nearly a mile and one-third; and at regatta time the Oxfordshire side of the river behind the flag posts is one vast assemblage of river steamers, house boats, and every description of pleasure boats, crowded with the gayest of aquatic costumes, the towing-path side being equally full of small boats and pedestrians. The racing lasts during three days, most of the trial heats being rowed on the first two days and the finals on the third; the boats from all parts of Great Britain, as well as from America, often put in an appearance as competitors for the different events.

The Post Office is in the Market Place, and is open on weekdays from 7 a.m. till 8.30 p.m.; on Sundays from 7 a.m. till 10 a.m., the last mail for London being at 8.15 p.m.; there is a pillar letter-box near the bridge.

Hotels – 'Red Lion', 'Angel', 'Catherine Wheel', 'Royal'.

Boats Housed or Let – Johnson & Peachey, A. Parrott, H. Clisby, Hobbs & Sons, H. Hooper.

Watermen – W. Vaughan, W. Parrott, Jun., T. Neal, E. Vaughan, C. Atkins, G. Neal, T. Potter, G. Reeves, G. Vaughan, J. James.

Fishing – The fishing at Henley (except about Regatta time when the immense traffic drives away the fish) is fairly good. Jack, perch, barbel and roach, not forgetting the lively gudgeon, being among the fish caught.

Fishermen – W. Parrott, E. Vaughan, W. Parrott, Sen., W. Vaughan, T. Potter, C. Atkins, T. Neal, G. Neal.

Bathing – At Solomon's Hatch.

From Lechlade to nearly a mile below Henley, the river forms the boundary between the counties of Oxford and Berks, but at Fawley Court, Buckinghamshire begins; the boundary line being a little above the house, which forms a striking object in the view. Remenham farm and village is on the opposite side of the river, and then comes Regatta or Temple Island with its miniature imitation of a Grecian temple. Not far below the Island, on the right bank, is Greenlands, the residence of the Right Hon W.H. Smith, with its white house partly hidden by trees. Greenlands was fortified in the time of the Civil War by its then owner, Sir John D'Oyley, for the King; and withstood a severe siege of nearly six months in 1644, when the house being almost destroyed the garrison was forced to surrender.

REGATTA ISLAND.

Greenlands

½

Temple or
Regatta I.

48 m.

Fawley

Court

Bucks
Oxon

Remenham

Fair Mile

Part of
Henley

MEDMENHAM ABBEY.

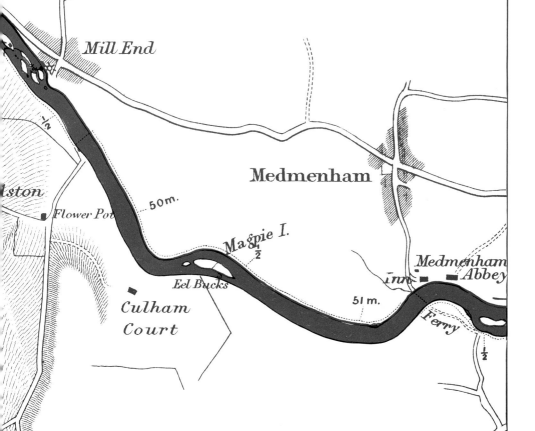

Mill End

Aston

Flower Pot

50 m.

Medmenham

Magpie I.
½

Eel Bucks

Culham
Court

51 m.

Inn

Medmenham
Abbey

Ferry

½

½

Hambledon Lock c. 1875

HAMBLEDON LOCK from Henley Bridge, *2 miles 2 furlongs 35 yards; to Medmenham Ferry, 2 miles 0 furlongs 66 yards: falls from 1 ft in high to 4 ft 8 in in low water; average in summer, about 4 ft*

The river at Hambledon is broken up by islands, between which the weirs are placed, and for a little distance the stream is rather sharp, making it advisable often to track up from Aston Ferry. The weir pools are good for jack and other large fish, and this sharp stream is noted for its gudgeon, which are said to reach a larger size here than any other swim on the river. Below the islands the river broadens out into a fine wide reach, which lasts until we get to the bend near Culham Court, a brick mansion with stone dressings, standing on the high ground on the right bank.

The little village of Aston stands back from the river. It is a pretty rural spot, and gives its name to the ferry over the river.
Hotel – The 'Flower Pot'.

At Magpie Island, a little further on, the right-hand stream is blocked up by some picturesque eel bucks; after passing this island the stream widens again, and continues until Medmenham is reached.

MEDMENHAM ABBEY from Hambledon *2 miles 0 furlong 66 yards; to Hurley Lock, 1 mile 4 furlongs 168 yards*

Medmenham Abbey is one of those places of general resort which please everyone. It is by far the most favourite rendezvous in the neighbourhood for out-door parties who journey up or down the river; and its charming position and quaint old buildings all help to make it worthy of the honour paid. A dance on its clean-shaved lawn in the twilight, or when the rising moon sheds her soft sweet light over the scene, casting such long weird shadows amongst the old buildings and cloisters as to make one look to see if some of the old monks are not hiding there, is a treat to be remembered, and at the earliest opportunity repeated. Medmenham Abbey was founded in the thirteenth century, as an offshoot to the monastery of Woburn in Bedfordshire, but did not prosper; and when the commissioners appointed by Henry came to inquire into its condition, it was found to have 'monks, two; servants, none; debts, none; woods, none; movable goods worth £1 3s. 8d., and the house wholly ruinous.' It was ordered to be appended to Bisham, and suffered to linger on for a few years longer, till the monasteries were entirely dissolved.

Medmenham Abbey from the Thames c. 1899

THE THAMES OF HENRY TAUNT

After this it was converted into a dwelling house, and so remained till – in the eighteenth century – it was utilized by the notorious Francis Dashwood, Lord de Despencer, and the other twelve members of the Franciscan order of mock-monks, who made the place notorious with their proceedings, which were the scandal of the neighbourhood. Their motto still exists over the doorway of the side tower, 'Fay ce que voudras' (Each as he likes), and the pages of Chrysal's *Adventures of a Guinea* contain an account of their shameless doings. The building has been improved by the addition of a ruinous tower at the corner facing the river; and being partly overgrown with ivy and other creepers, it forms, with the magnificent trees which shade it, one of the most complete pictures on the Thames.

Hotel – The 'Ferry'.

Fishing – The reaches here, both up and down, are good for chub and pike, and at Harleyford Weir are fine perch. At the islands below Medmenham are fine swims, and from here right up to Culham Court the water is deep and teeming with fish.

Fisherman – R. Young.

Passing down from Medmenham a group of islands is soon reached, beautifully decorated in the autumn with white water-lilies in the eddies, and purple loosestrife, as well as numerous other waterside plants round the banks; a little lower, numerous beds of reeds cover over the sides of the stream with their luxurious growth, standing up from the river several feet in height. And now begins a bold range of chalk cliffs, partially covered with foliage, and the river widens out into a clear lake-like piece of water till New Lock weir is reached. When nearing the overfall *keep closely to the right hand towing-path bank*, at all events in high water time, *as the weir directly faces the centre of the stream*, and the draught from it is very great at times. Through the open part of the weir, and down the back water, was the navigable waterway in olden times; and close to the cottages stands the old capstan, which was then used to force the barges up the fall against the rush of the stream.

On the heights is Danesfield, with its remains of a Danish camp. The house, called after the camp, Danesfield, the seat of Scott Murray, Esq., is in the Italian style, and has appended a handsome chapel (Catholic), with fine sculptured reredos, and the interior beautifully decorated. A pretty Swiss châlet is erected on the grounds near the river. The way up the cliffs from the cottages is by the path of a hundred steps. From the top an extensive view all over the valley is obtained, with the islands of the river and their silver streams between, and in the middle distance the village of Hurley forms a notable object in the landscape. In the backwater are some lovely wooded bits for the

127

Hurley Lock and mill c. 1890

artist, the old dilapidated eel bucks, with their stage of broken woodwork, and the river plants springing up around the base of the piles on which they stand; here and there a tree partly down across a stream, and leaning its weight on others; whilst, out of the dense foliage, the swift flying kingfisher darts like a flash of coloured lightning as he skims over the sparkling water beneath. Harleyford House, the seat of Sir W.R. Clayton, stands just below, sheltered behind by its beautiful hanging woods.

HURLEY

HURLEY LOCK from Medmenham Ferry *1 mile 4 furlongs 168 yards; to Temple Lock, 5 furlongs 23 yards: average fall about 2 ft 8 in; does not vary much*

Hurley has a number of very interesting old remains, and if time can be spared a visit should be made. There are the remains of the old Benedictine Monastery of our Lady, founded by Geoffery Mandeville, one of the Norman knights of William the Conqueror; the church being entire, and the western door in good preservation.

Close by is the old refectory, which was formed into the stables for the mansion, built on the site of the old monastery, and called, after it, Lady Place. Only the vaults of this mansion remain; but these vaults, which were said to have been originally the burial-place of the monastery, have a large amount of interest attached to their few remains. In the reign of Elizabeth the mansion was built here by the then owner of the estate, Sir Richard Lovelace, who was afterwards, by King Charles, created Lord Lovelace of Hurley. During the latter part of the reign of Charles II, and that of James, this house was the meeting-place of those dissatisfied with the state of things at that time, and favourable to the Prince of Orange. These meetings were held under cover of a round of splendid hospitalities, the most secret consultations being held in the vaults, where measures were adopted that led to the Revolution of 1688; the requisition inviting the Prince of Orange to come over being signed in the little recess at the farther end.

These vaults were visited by the King after his accession to the throne, and also by George III and his Queen in 1785. Some other remains of the extensive monastic buildings are plainly seen in the large barns, etc., in the village, which also contains some old houses, one having a very picturesque porch.
Hotel – The 'Old Bell'.

The Old Bell Inn, Hurley, c. 1890

TEMPLE AND BISHAM

TEMPLE LOCK from Hurley *5 furlongs 23 yards; to Marlow Bridge, 1 mile 3 furlongs 201 yards: falls from about 2 ft 3 in in high to 4 ft 9 in in low water; average in summer, about 4 ft 6 in*

A little way below Hurley Lock the different streams all unite in a broad reach of water, and facing is Temple House, the seat of General Owen Williams, and on the other side, its little house prettily embosomed in the feathery foliage of some large beech trees, is the pretty Temple Lock.   Just below the lock is a fine new weir, built mostly of blocks of concrete; Temple Mills follow, and then Bisham Grange, very pleasantly situated, facing the river.

Bisham Abbey, close below, is now the seat of H. Vansittart-Neale, Esq.; in the time of Stephen it belonged to the Knights Templars, who built a refectory here. This order having been dissolved, it passed into the hands of the Augustine monks; and when the smaller religious houses were dissolved Bisham had a revenue of £357 4s. 6d. It was then refounded for the Benedictines, who were shortly after suppressed, and in the time of Elizabeth it was in the possession of the Hoby family, by whom the greater part of the present mansion was erected.

Elizabeth herself is stated to have spent part of her life here, in the custody, or under the care, of Lady Hoby. This house, like many others erected about this period, has amongst its other rooms a beautiful hall, with half-timbered Gothic roof, and high oak-panelled wainscoting, and is embellished with family portraits. It is also the scene of a ghost story, told, with 'bated breath, of Lady Hoby, who – without her head, – walks here in stately splendour at the witching hour of night, as a punishment for beating one of her children to death for blotting his copybook.

Bisham Church stands close to the river, and its fine old Norman tower peeps between the stately poplars which partly shade it. The interior presents a pleasing appearance, and contains, amongst others, a beautiful altar tomb to the Hoby family, with monumental effigies, one of which (a junior) is laid on its side at Lady Hoby's feet, and is pointed out as the boy she killed. This part of the river is the Marlow Regatta course; and a short distance round the bend is Marlow Bridge and Church.

BISHAM ABBEY.

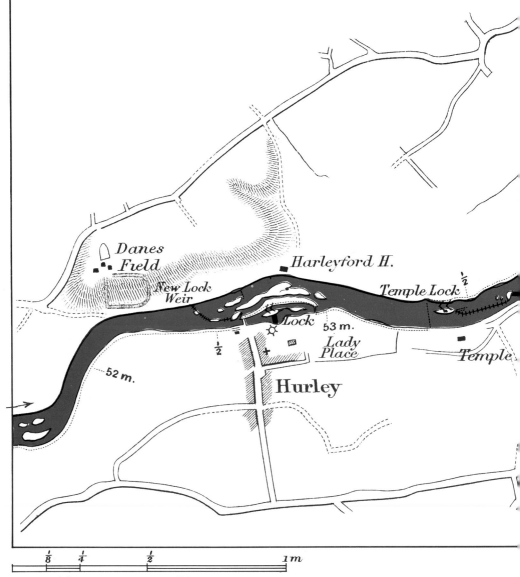

Danes
Field

Harleyford H.

New Lock
Weir

Temple Lock

½

Lock

53 m.

½

Lady
Place

Temple

52 m.

Hurley

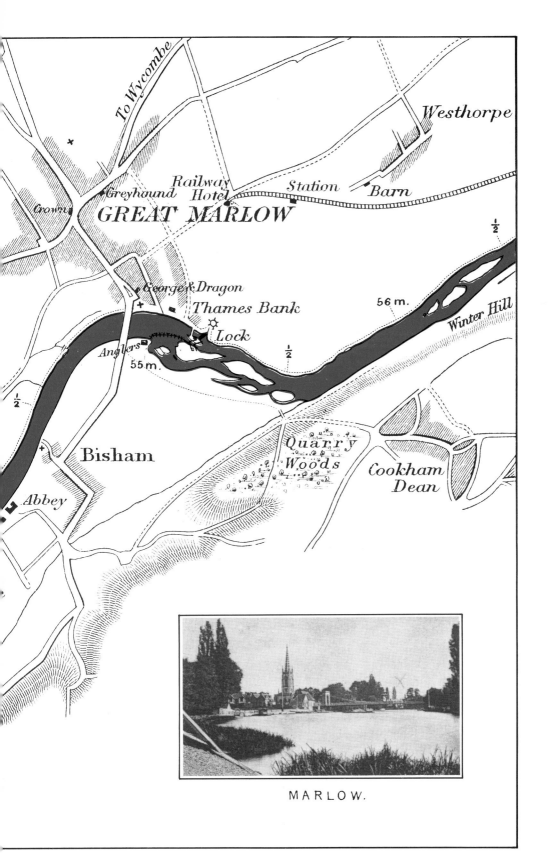

To Wycombe

Westhorpe

Railway Hotel

Station

Barn

Greyhound

Crown

GREAT MARLOW

George & Dragon

Thames Bank

Lock

$\frac{1}{2}$

56 m.

Winter Hill

Anglers

55 m.

$\frac{1}{2}$

$\frac{1}{2}$

Bisham

Quarry Woods

Cookham Dean

Abbey

MARLOW.

GREAT MARLOW

MARLOW BRIDGE from Temple Lock *1 mile 3 furlongs 201 yards;*
to Cookham Bridge, 3 miles 7 furlongs 158 yards

Railway Station – GWR, about 3 furlongs from the bridge.

Marlow is a clean little town, but has in itself few distinctive features besides its broad straight High Street, leading up past the church from the bridge. The greater part of the charms of Marlow lie clustered round the river, where the graceful suspension bridge, the flowing weir, and the spire and chancel of the church, make many a scene not to be lightly passed by.

The Suspension Bridge was erected in 1835, and is undoubtedly a great ornament to the river. It replaced an old wooden pile bridge (which stood just below), the scene of the laughable story of the Puppy Pie; from which sprang the orthodox salutation to every Marlow man – 'Where did you eat Puppy Pies last?'* The grand old weir has lately been rebuilt in terraces of concrete blocks; and although, no doubt, better for its stability, it will not compare with the falling water of the old form. The church is a bad specimen of nineteenth century Gothic, although the spire has a few redeeming features; but lately a new chancel has been added from the designs of the late Sir G.G. Scott, and at a future time it is intended to complete the body of the church in the same style. This new design is a very beautiful specimen in the Decorated style of architecture, and will be a great ornament to the river when built.

Marlow boasts also a Catholic church in St Peter's Street, from the designs of Pugin, and a pretty little church (Trinity) at the north end of the town.

The Post Office is in West Street, and is open on week days from 7.30 a.m. till 8.30 p.m.; on Sundays from 7.30 a.m. till 10 a.m.: the last mail for London leaving at 7.50 p.m. There is a pillar box in the wall leading up from the bridge.

Hotels – The 'Anglers', just below the bridge, The 'George and Dragon', High

---

* The story behind 'Puppy Pies' refers to a certain landlord of an inn in Maidenhead who learnt that a group of bargemen intended to raid his larder one evening. In anticipation of this act he took a litter of recently drowned puppies and baked these in a pie. The robbers, it is understood, took this to eat near Marlow Bridge, and feasted on what they thought was rabbit pie.

St., The 'Fisherman's Retreat', St Peter's St., The 'Greyhound', The 'Crown'.

Boats Housed or Let – Shaw and Sons, Meakes and Redknap, on Berkshire side, J. Cannon, at the bridge.

Fishing – Marlow is one of the best places for all-round fishing on the river. There are plenty of trout in the weir pool, and also in the reach below Temple and Bisham and at Quarry Woods. Jack abound in the reaches above the bridge, Quarry Woods, and the Chalk pit. Perch, roach, and barbel are found both above and below the lock, whilst gudgeon, chub, and dace are nearly everywhere.

Fishermen – W. Shaw, G. White, G. White, Jun., W. Thorpe, H. Rockwell, T. Barnes, G. Coster, J. Rockwell, W. Coster.

Bathing – Below the weir; from the 'Anglers'; and also below the lock.

MARLOW LOCK *1 furlong 107 yards beyond the bridge: falls from 1 ft 6 in in high to 6 ft 6 in in low water; average in summer, about 5 ft 6 in*

In high water keep clear of the weir above, and on leaving the lock below care must be taken to guard against the rush of the water from the Mill. From the lock to Quarry Corner is a swift stream, and in going up it is often advisable to tow, especially if the boat be a heavy one.

Quarry Woods is the Marlow walk; and a favoured spot it is, particularly in the autumn, when the beech trees are coloured with their gorgeous tints, or in the sultry summer's day, when a lounge in a hammock stretched from tree to tree is a perfect luxury. These woods stretch from the Bisham Road to Winter Hill, a distance of more than a mile, and the beautiful paths that lead through them are open to the public.

A path leads across the fields from the Bisham side of Marlow Bridge to the woods, which it enters by means of a picturesque little footbridge over a rippling stream, and is continued up the steep hill-side on to Cookham Dean, or by side walks through the length of the woods.

The conditions under which landing is allowed is as follows:

Application must be made in writing to Mr Morton, Abbey Farm, Great Marlow, specifying the date for which permission is asked, and the number of the party. If permission is granted, the following conditions must be compiled with:– The order allowing landing must be shown if demanded; litter of every sort must be removed; and care must be taken not to injure the trees, shrubs, etc. As regards camping out, special permission will be necessary; and application should be made some time beforehand, specifying names and addresses of persons wishing to camp.

It should be understood that Mr Vansittart-Neale does not occupy Quarry Cottage or the wood below it.

It is hoped that everyone allowed to use the woods will not abuse the favour (as some have already done), or leave marks of devastation or *debris* behind them. It is really very bad form to do these things, and thus help to shut up the most enjoyable spots on the river.

A bluff in the wood called Lady Winifred's Seat, from which a fine view of Marlow is obtained, is said to have been the scene of a tragical legend in connection with one of the monks of Bisham and a lady of the neighbourhood, who were eloping together. They were followed in hot pursuit by the father of the lady, and took refuge here to escape from him, but, refusing to come down when summoned, he, in his rage, fired, and unfortunately killed the lady, who died in her lover's arms.

BOURNE END

Bourne End is a pleasant little straggling village near the end of the Wyke Stream or Bourne. The GWR (Wycombe branch) crosses the river by a dilapidated-looking wooden bridge, the station, situated about 3 furlongs from the landing place above the bridge, being the junction for the short branch rail to Marlow.

At Horsham's boat yard is the mouth of the little Bourne, rising in the watercress beds a short distance above; and below Abney House at the large Paper Mill, whose tall chimney rears itself above the surroundings, the river receives the waters of the Wyke, which stream, rising near West Wycombe, flows down the valley, driving more mills in its course than many a more imposing river. It is noted in its upper part for its trout, and its waters are preserved by a local angling society, who have their headquarters at High Wycombe.

Boats Housed or Let – Horsham & Co.
Hotels – 'Railway', close to station, 'Red Lion'.
Fisherman, and Boats to Let – D. Brown.

COOKHAM.

LLEWELLYN'S HOTEL.

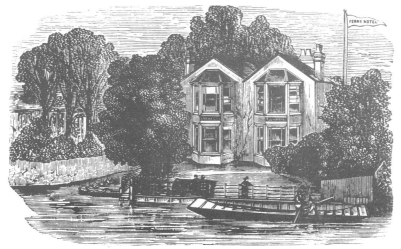

CLOSE BELOW THE BRIDGE.

This Hotel having been extensively enlarged, offers superior accommodation to Anglers, Boating Parties, and others visiting this the finest part of the Thames.

Choice Wines and Spirits.

BOATS, PUNTS, & CANOES TO LET BY THE HOUR, DAY, WEEK, OR SEASON,
ON REASONABLE TERMS.

JAMES LLEWELLYN, Proprietor.

H. & S. ROSE,

RIVERSIDE, MAIDENHEAD,

BOAT, PUNT, AND CANOE BUILDERS.

A Large Stock of New and Second-hand Boats for Sale or Hire
by the Day, Month, or Season.

BOATS HOUSED, REPAIRED, OR VARNISHED.

Telegraphic Address:—ROSE, BOATBUILDER, MAIDENHEAD.

Railway Hotel

Spade Oak

57 m.

Spade Oak
Ferry ½

Bourne End
Station

Abney
House

R. Wyke

Bourne End

58 m

½

Cookham +

Ferry Hotel

King's Arms

59 m.

Odney Weir

Loc

Formos

Cookham Station

Fer

60 m

½

AT THE SPRING _ CLIVEDEN.

CLIVEDEN – COTTAGE & WOODS.

CLIVEDEN HOUSE.

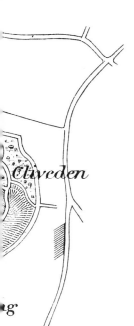

AT THE FERRY – CLIVEDEN.

Cookham Lock c. 1880

COOKHAM

COOKHAM BRIDGE from Marlow Lock *3 miles 6 furlongs 51 yards; to Cookham Lock, 4 furlongs*
COOKHAM LOCK to Boulter's Lock *1 mile 7 furlongs 112 yards; falls from 1 ft 6 in in high to 5 ft in low water; average in summer, about 4 ft*

Station – GWR, Wycombe branch, 5 furlongs from the bridge.

Cookham is another favourite stopping place, and the scenery of this district, including as it does Cliveden, rivals any other on the river. Cookham Church stands nearly close to the river above the bridge, and its ivy mantled tower forms a pretty centre-piece to the view when coming down the river. It is mostly Early English, and built partly of flint with rather a tasteful porch on its south front. There is a fine view from its tower looking over Hedsor and Cliveden, and also up the river to Bourne End and Little Marlow.

Cookham has a slim iron toll-bridge, built in 1867 (replacing an old picturesque wooden structure), which stretches across the river just above where it divides into four streams, which again unite at Cliveden. The cut to the lock is the second of these, counting from the left or Bucks shore, the first being the weir stream, and the third and fourth leading respectively to Odney Weir and the Mill.

The view from the bridge is very good, ranging in a panorama the streams with the hills beyond, in the distance being an old sham castle, on Hedsor Hill, called the Folly, which has an imposing look from this spot.

Cookham is a pleasant little village in which there are some picturesque old cottages, its one street leads on to a moor, where geese disport themselves in great numbers, and the moor leads onward to the railway station, over a causeway and wooden bridge. From the village lovely walks and drives lead through Cookham Dean and Bisham Woods to Marlow, or along pleasant Buckinghamshire lanes to Hedsor, Dropmore, and Burnham, with roads bordered with wild flowers in the greatest profusion, the foxglove, wild hyacinth, heather, and honeysuckle, in their season, scenting the air and delighting the eye with their varied beauty.

Boats to be Let or Housed – J. Llewellyn, W. Lacey.
Hotels – The 'Ferry', close to the bridge, The 'King's Arms'.

Cookham Lock on Bank Holiday c. 1890

Watermen – J. Pym; T. Wigg; A. Hatch.

Fishing – Cookham reach is a splendid water for perch, roach, and jack, with good trout; the Cookham, Maidenhead, and Bray Angling Association, having turned in a large stock of the latter. Fish are often caught, indeed it is very seldom that in passing, one does not see a number of anglers in their punts, moored in the characteristic way of the Thames. Below, under the Cliveden woods, the water is still good and well stocked. Barbel and gudgeon are often plentiful, and good pitches may be found every now and then the whole distance to Boulter's Weir.

Fishermen – W. Jones; Ed. Godden; H. Wilder, of Maidenhead (generally here in the season).

Bathing – At Odney Weir, which may be reached by a path from the lower end of the village. Caution should be used in bathing in weir pools in high water time, as then eddies exist in which the strongest swimmer is powerless; and in all places, unless the bather be a good swimmer, it is wise to make oneself thoroughly acquainted with the particular spot and its peculiarities, before plunging into the water. Most of the weir pools on the Thames are capital places for a bathe to the strong swimmer, but timid ones ought in every case to take the necessary precautions against danger, by bathing only in company, and knowing the run of the place.

From Cookham Bridge and Ferry, the lock cut made about 1830, leads us under a light iron bridge to the Lock, one of the prettiest on the river, passing which, we in a few moments join the main stream, and are amidst the grand loveliness of the Cliveden Woods. Hedsor, the seat of Lord Boston, occupies the first part of the hill, and includes the backwater below Cookham Weir to the eel-bucks; the road to Hedsor and its picturesque little church leads over Cookham bridge; the footpath across the fields turns out just over the bridge. Behind Hedsor is Dropmore, noted for its grand variety of trees – permission to walk or drive through the grounds is readily obtained, and when the rhododendrons are in full flower the scene is extremely beautiful.

CLIVEDEN AND FORMOSA

Cliveden is pre-eminently the grandest reach on the Thames, with its hills and hanging woods stretching up from the river's edge. The moment we reach the main stream below the lock this magnificent scenery bursts on our view, the first object of interest being the very picturesque Ferry Cottage, with the

Cliveden Reach looking upstream with the eel-buck stage in the distance c. 1888

lower weir of Hedsor filling up and breaking the line of the river. The towing-path here is a lovely walk under the overhanging trees, and edged with many bright riverside flowers; from it and the river some beautiful views of the lovely Formosa Island are obtained. This island, which lies opposite to Cliveden, is not without beauty in its magnificent trees; but its situation in relation to the views obtained of the Cliveden Woods, and the lake-like stream which runs at its feet, is the finest on the river. At the end of the reach the towing-path crosses to the other side of the river again by another ferry, the view from which place, looking up the river, is in every way beautiful; the principal object being the cottage belonging to the ferry.

A little distance onward below the spring the river is divided into two streams by some pretty tree-covered islands, partly edged with rushes, and from here we get our first glimpse on the river of Cliveden House, as it seemingly nestles in a dell between the hills, and, as we row down, this grand palatial mansion more fully reveals itself, forming the centrepiece to many lovely combinations of hill and dell and luxuriant foliage among this richest of beautiful landscapes – a panorama of extraordinary grandeur.

Cliveden House stands on a broad platform of tableland, which extends some distance beyond it to Hedsor; in front of the house a fine bold terrace extends itself across, the views from which are extremely magnificent, unequalled elsewhere on the Thames. Cliveden House is a beautiful classic structure from the designs of Barry, and stands on the site of the one destroyed by fire. The main front looks out upon the terrace; but the entrance is on the opposite side, up the grand avenue of lime trees. The clock tower is also a graceful building, and its pretty chimes make music which echoes through the wooded glades on the river's banks. Cliveden House was first erected by Villiers, Duke of Buckingham, of whom Dryden says:

> A man so various that he seemed to be
> Not one, but all mankind's epitome.

Pope speaks of the house as:

> Cliefden's proud alcove,
> The bower of wanton Shrewsbury and love . . .

in which he refers to a well-known episode in the life of Villiers, and his connection with the Countess of Shrewsbury, whose husband he killed in a duel. Cliveden was afterwards for some time the summer residence of

Frederick, Prince of Wales, the father of George III. The masque of *Alfred* by Thomson, was written for him, and first performed here; but is now entirely forgotten except one immortal song – 'Rule Britannia'. The seat now belongs to the Duke of Westminster. The house is not open to the public.

Returning to the river, which divides itself into four streams – the left-hand one forms the Taplow Mill head, the broader middle stream goes to Boulter's Weir and Ray Mills, and the right-hand cut leads to Boulter's Lock.

Boulter's Weir has lately been rebuilt and considerably enlarged, the water-way being augmented by a side overflow which, in flood time, carries over an enormous volume of water. This being the case, boats should steer clear of passing down to the danger board, and in entering or leaving the cut, be careful to hug the towing-path shore.

The hills continue, forming the grounds of Taplow Court, the top of whose turrets just peep over the trees. Taplow Court is a modern built house of red brick with stone dressings, in good taste.

BOULTER'S LOCK AND RAY MEAD

BOULTER'S LOCK from Cliveden Ferry 1 mile 3 furlongs 178 yards; to Maidenhead Bridge, 5 furlongs 70 yards: falls from 3 ft in high to 7 ft 6 in in low water; average in summer, about 6 ft 6 in

Boulter's is perhaps the busiest lock on the river, and on Bank holidays the crush in the lock is a sight to be seen, some twenty or more small boats, with perhaps a steam launch or two, are crammed in with the result that the greatest care and watermanship are needed to get through safely. Accidents, however, very seldom happen, although over 800 boats have been known to pass through in the day.

The riverside at Ray Mead, along to Maidenhead Bridge, has grown very fashionable within the last few years. The road is dotted with villa residences, and two good hotels stand on the bank. The scene is very pleasant – on the further bank being Glenisland, the seat of Sir R. Palmer, with Taplow Woods behind it, and the foreground is nearly always enlivened with a variety of passing craft. The stream is swift right down to the bridge, and it is often wise to track when coming up instead of rowing.

Hotels – 'Ray Mead', close to Boulter's Lock, 'New Thames', on the riverside.

Boats to be Let and Housed – W. Deacon, H. Woodhouse, H. and S. Rose, H. Wilder and Son, E. Andrews.

Ponies for towing – At Deacon's, 'Ray Mead' Hotel.

Fishing – The fishing to Boulter's is good for chub, and there are also some capital swims for gudgeon and barbel. Below Maidenhead Bridge, jack and perch abound. Barbel also are found in quantities, while along the whole distance of the osier beds chub are in great force, and other fish are to be met with. A quantity of trout are yearly turned in by the association, and many of them are grown fine fish, so that the trout fishing in these waters has grown very successful, and fish are plentiful.

Fishermen – Hy. Wilder, H. Wilder, Jun., Ed. Andrews, M. Andrews, Geo. Winn, E. Winn, B. Clark, J. Gill, L. Wilder C. Andrews, C. Taplin.

Fish – Trout, jack, perch, chub, roach, dace, barbel, etc.

Railway Station – See Maidenhead.

MAIDENHEAD BRIDGE AND MAIDENHEAD

MAIDENHEAD BRIDGE from Boulter's Lock *5 furlongs 70 yards; to Bray Lock, 1 mile 3 furlongs 152 yards*

Stations – Maidenhead (GWR, main line; also junction for Marlow branch), about a mile from the bridge. TAPLOW (GWR) is also about a mile along the London Road.

The Western Road, to Reading, Bath, etc., passes over Maidenhead Bridge, a well-built stone structure of some thirteen circular arches altogether. Just below it the Great Western Railway passes over a fine bridge, with two elliptical archs spanning the whole of the river – one of Brunel's grand designs. One of the arches has a fine echo under it:

> Ha, ha! ha, ha! from summit to ridge,
> A laugh was the echo of Maidenhead Bridge.

Hotel – 'Skindle's'.

Boats Housed and to Let – J. Bond.

Maidenhead is a growing town extending mostly along the Western Road for over a mile. Within the last few years an enormous extension has taken

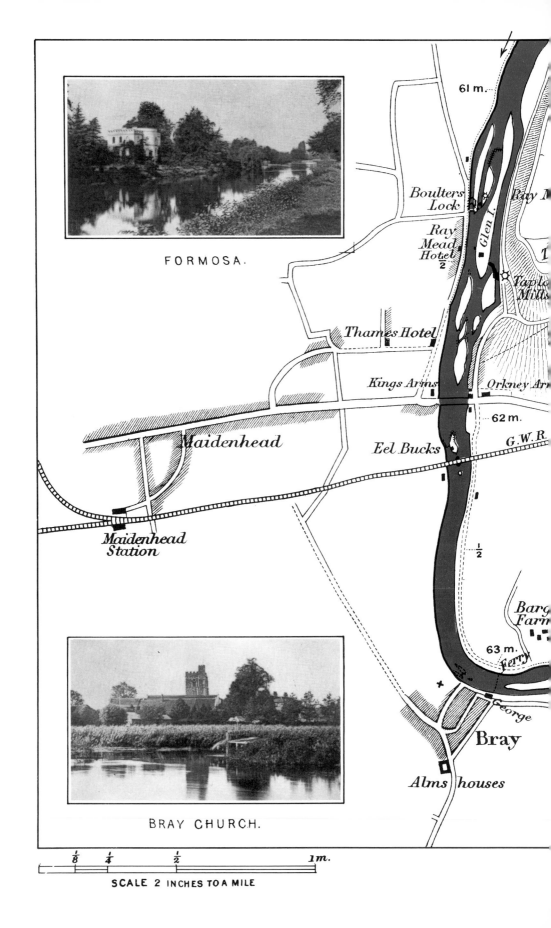

FORMOSA.

61 m.

Boulters
Lock

Glen I.

Ray M

Ray
Mead
Hotel
2

Taplo
Mills

Thames Hotel

1

Kings Arms

Orkney Ar

62 m.

Maidenhead

Eel Bucks

G.W.R

Maidenhead
Station

1
2

Barg
Farm

63 m.

Ferry

George

Bray

+

Alms houses

BRAY CHURCH.

SCALE 2 INCHES TO A MILE

1
8
1
4
1
2
1 m.

View at RAY MEAD.

To London

MAIDENHEAD BRIDGE.

Amerden
Bank

64 m.

TAPLOW BRIDGE &c.

Maidenhead Bridge c. 1886

place, new streets, new churches, a new town hall, etc., having sprung up in several directions from the main road.

Maidenhead is, no doubt, the corruption of Mayden-hythe (the Maiden's Wharf), and really stands partly in Bray and partly in Cookham parishes. It was years ago an old market town, when its inns were numerous and large for the accommodation of the numerous coaches which passed through on their way to London or the west.

In July 1647 the unfortunate Charles I was permitted to meet his children here after a separation of several years. The town was decorated with green boughs and strewed with flowers in honour of the occasion, and the children were allowed to drive with him to Caversham where they remained for two days.

Of the churches, the one at Boyne Hill, a rather florid but tasteful edifice of red and white brick with detached tower and lofty spire, is the finest. It stands on the rising ground overlooking the town to the west.

The Post Office is situated in the centre of the High Street, and is open on week days from 7 a.m. till 9.45 p.m., at which time the box closes for all parts. There is a pillar box close to the bridge.

Hotels and Inns – 'Bear', 'Cliveden', 'Saracen's head', etc.

One of the pleasantest trips in this neighbourhood is that to Burnham Beeches. The Corporation of the City of London deserve thanks for preserving for the public these exquisite remains of a grand old forest of beech trees, the place *par excellence* for picnic and pleasure parties; and very few days pass in the summer without several large gatherings being found there. The beeches have mostly been polled (tradition says this was done by Cromwell's soldiers), and have grown into a collection of rugged, gnarled boles and roots, so weird in their outlines, that by moonlight the appearance of any number of ghostly figures can readily be imagined. An extremely pleasant outing can be spent here, the place being easily reached by road either from Cookham or Maidenhead.

BRAY

Bray, the mother parish of Maidenhead, is at the end of the broad reach leading from Maidenhead Bridge. The church is the attraction not only from its beautiful architecture but from the memory of its vicar – Simon Aleyn – who, more than once, bowing to the changes of the times, gave rise to the

The tow-path near Maidenhead Bridge c. 1890

celebrated political song, 'The Vicar of Bray'.* The combination of the church and the eel bucks seen from the river, is very picturesque, as is also the scene looking down to the ferry.

Bray is a grand old church, mostly in the Decorated style of architecture, and it is well worth the time to see it from the churchyard. It consists of a fine long nave and chancel, with large aisles stretching nearly the whole length; and the massive square tower, with corner buttresses reaching to the top, standing distinct, but connected with the church, seems to tower above and crown the whole. In the interior is kept a 'Foxe's Book of Martyrs', to which a chain is attached, a relic of olden times, when these books were chained to a pillar of the church. There are some very good memorial brasses, amongst them one to the celebrated vicar.

On the western side of the churchyard are some old picturesque half-timbered houses and lych-gate, the choice bits of many an artist of fame, and in the village the church tower in one place peeps lovingly over the houses, and forms another subject for a picture.

We must not leave Bray without visiting the Jesus Hospital, a few yards down the road towards Windsor, founded by William Goddard, in the time of Queen Elizabeth, for a number of poor occupants, and now kept up by the Fishmongers Company of London. These picturesque buildings are arranged in the form of a square, the chapel on the farther side of the quadrangle facing the entrance gate, over which is a statue of the founder.

Hotel – 'The George'.

Boats to be Let and Housed – H. Woodhouse. See also under Maidenhead. W.C. Mickley, at the 'George' Ferry.

BRAY LOCK from Maidenhead Bridge, *1 mile 3 furlongs 152 yards; to Monkey Island, 4 furlongs 128 yards: average fall about 3 ft*

Bray Lock has been entirely rebuilt on the Bucks shore, and slightly lower down than the old lock was; a new weir is also in course of construction a little

---

* 'The Vicar of Bray' is the famous eighteenth century song, by an unknown author, of the vicar who boasted that he would accommodate himself to the religious views of whichever monarch was on the throne. It is thought to refer to Symon Symonds, the Vicar of Bray under four Tudor monarchs, who was 'twice a Papist and twice a Protestant'.

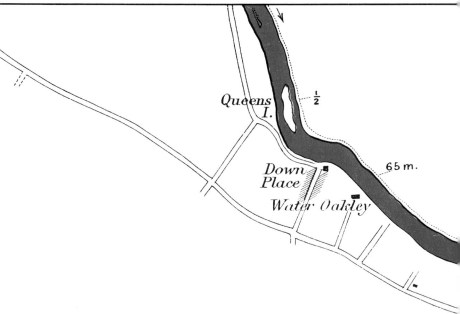

Queens
I.

Down
Place

Water Oakley

½

65 m.

MONKEY ISLAND.

WATER OAKLEY COURT.

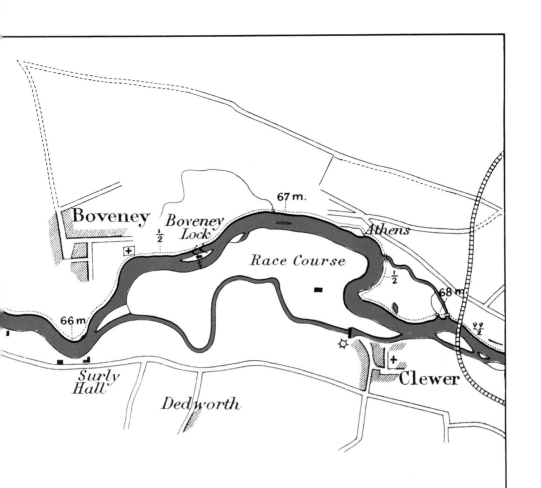

Boveney

Boveney
Lock

½

67 m.

Athens

Race Course

½

68 m.

66 m

½

Surly
Hall

Dedworth

Clewer

WINDSOR CASTLE.

below the old one. The average fall of the lock is now about 3 ft, but will in all probability exceed this when the new weir is finished. A sad accident occurred at the weir on 15 May 1886, by which three lives were lost and others only saved by the exertions of the lock-keeper, Morris, his son, and daughter; for which they received the bronze medal and thanks of the Royal Humane Society.

Fishing – The fishing round Bray is good for jack, perch, and gudgeon; barbel are found at the weir and in the stream near Monkey Island; and chub exist nearly everywhere, under the shelving banks on the one side of the river, and the osier-beds on the other.

Fishermen – J. Chapman, W. Morris; Jun.; R. Plummer Jun.

Below Bray is the swifest stream on the Thames, and it is always advisable to track up from the corner near Down Place to the lock. On our way we pass Monkey Island Hotel, which is named from a room the ceiling of which is covered with paintings representing monkeys at various sports; it was erected by the third Duke of Marlborough, to whom the island belonged. The towing-path above Monkey Island belongs to the farm above, the owners of which have the right to supply the necessary horses to tow up a barge or boat, charging 5s. for each horse required.

Below Monkey Island is Queen's Island, at the end of which at the turn is Down Place, once the headquarters of the celebrated Kit-Cat Club, who, under the guise of jollity and wit, were united for a higher purpose – the defence of the House of Hanover. Water Oakley Court follows, a pleasant modern castellated building, half covered with greenery, with grounds sloping down to the river, and a water-wheel jutting out in the stream, used for raising water from the river.

A little below we come to 'Surley Hall'. This is a well-known stopping-place for the Eton boys, and where in a meadow opposite they hold their annual College Festival on the 4 June, including a procession of boats.

The little hamlet of Boveney opposite consists of a picturesque court and one or two groups of pretty half-timbered cottages in a very pleasant lane, with the church, which stands close to the river in a little green enclosure of hedgerow and trees. It is a quaint little edifice, with a white wooden bell turret at the western end, containing three bells, whose voices, the villagers say, cry 'Come-to-Church'. The interior is thoroughly rustic, with great beams crossing overhead from side to side; the roughly-carved pulpit and screen, with the seats, are evidently from the hand of the village carpenter; and even the clumsy old lock bolted to the oak door, with its heavy key still bearing the marks of the file, are rustic work.

Fishing – Near Queen's Island are barbel and chub. Ekyn's pool, near the Willows, is good for pike and perch, and in many other places, easily spotted, fish of nearly every class abound, with the addition of trout, which now seem to be thriving in every suitable reach on the river.

BOVENEY LOCK from Bray Lock *3 miles 1 furlong 128 yards; to Windsor Bridge, 1 mile 7 furlongs 90 yards; falls from 2 ft 6 in in high to 4 ft in low water; average in summer, 3 ft 9 in*

Close behind the lock is the weir, the pool forming a splendid bathing place for good swimmers; and here is the first distant peep of the Royal Castle of Windsor, which now will be the centrepiece of all the scenes on the way down. On the right lies Windsor racecourse, and, a little way below, Athens, another well-known bathing-place for the Eton boys; then a sharp double curve brings us in sight of Clewer Church, with its beautiful graveyard and shingle-covered spire. A short distance forward is the Bow and String Iron Bridge, a splendid specimen of engineering skill, over which the Great Western Railway crosses the river, with its branch from Windsor to Slough.

Under the railway the grand old clump of elms on the Brocas* displays itself, and then Windsor Castle bursts out in all its magnificence, each bend of the river presenting it in a new position, and manifold combinations succeeding each other with every fresh beauty and grace. The view of Windsor Castle from the river is the grandest on the Thames.

WINDSOR AND ETON

WINDSOR BRIDGE from Boveney Lock *1 mile 7 furlongs 90 yards; to Romney Lock, 3 furlongs 96 yards*

Windsor Castle has grown with our national history, it having been commenced by William the Conqueror, who turned the neighbouring country into a royal forest, probably using the house as a hunting lodge. Henry I rebuilt and

---

* The name is derived from the Brocas family of Beaurepaire in France. Sir Bernard Brocas fought at Poitiers and was later MP for Hampshire for thirty years. The land on the Thames, after passing through various hands, was acquired by Henry Bost, Provost of Eton from 1477 to 1504, who left it to Eton College.

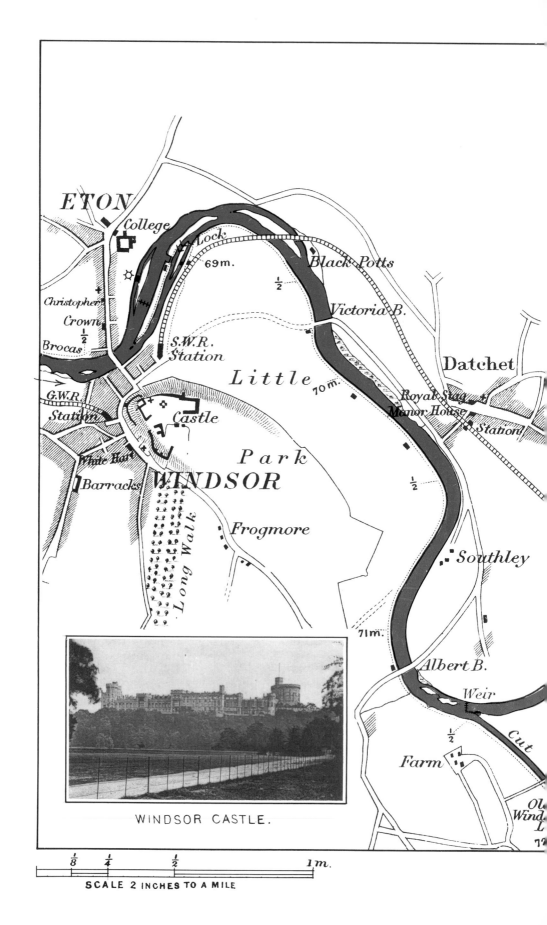

ETON

College

Lock

69 m.

Black Potts

½

Victoria B.

Datchet

Christopher

Crown

½

Brocas

S.W.R. Station

Little

70 m.

Royal Stag

Manor House

Station

G.W.R. Station

Castle

Park

White Hart

Barracks

WINDSOR

Frogmore

½

Long Walk

Southley

71 m.

Albert B.

Weir

½

Cut

Farm

Ol. Wind. L. 72

WINDSOR CASTLE.

SCALE 2 INCHES TO A MILE

⅛ ¼ ½ 1 m.

ETON COLLEGE.

OLD WINDSOR LOCK.

THE BELLS OF OUSELEY.

raised walls and ramparts round, making it one of his residences, and in a chapel which he built he celebrated his second marriage. In the time of Stephen the castle had advanced in strength till it was accounted the second in the kingdom. Henry II held a parliament in it, and it was seized by John on hearing the news of the imprisonment of his brother Richard. The barons besieged him here without success. It was a favourite residence with both Edward I and Edward II; but to Edward III, who was born here, we owe the greater part of its magnificence. William of Wykeham, the founder of Winchester College, was appointed Surveyor of the Works, and his design nearly equalled the present building in magnitude. Wykeham's salary was 'One shilling per day, and sixpence for his clerk,' but the workmen were impressed by the sheriffs of the surrounding counties, and compelled to work at the King's wages. This impressment went on from 1356 to 1374, and then ceased. In this reign the Order of the Garter was established; and the meetings of the order were held in the castle, which also saw John, King of France, and David of Scotland prisoners.

St George's Chapel was the next important addition, built in the reign of Edward IV, nearly a century after the former buildings. This exquisite specimen of Perpendicular architecture, one of the choicest gems of the whole pile, was designed by Richard Beauchamp, Bishop of Salisbury, and, after his death, completed by Sir Reginald Bray, who also built Henry VII's Chapel at Westminster.

Additions were made by both Henry VII and Henry VIII; but to Elizabeth we owe perhaps more than either of these former Sovereigns. She caused the North Terrace to be constructed, the view from which is one of the finest near the river, and extends far and wide; and she also caused Shakespeare to write his comedy of the *Merrie Wives of Windsor*, which was first performed before her here in 1593. Few alterations or additions of note took place during the reigns that followed, but in 1824 a complete restoration was begun. Parliament voted money towards the expenses, and the work proceeded, some £800,000 being laid out on the buildings and decorations, under the direction of Sir J. Wyatville.

Rebuilding and renovating is still going on, one of the latest works being the refacing etc., of the Curfew Tower, which stands boldly out in every view from the Brocas.

The arrangements for Windsor Castle are as follows:–

St George's Chapel is open between half-past 12 and 4 daily (except Wddnesdays), Divine Service being held at 10.30 and 3; on Sundays at 11 and 5.

THE THAMES OF HENRY TAUNT

The Royal Stables are open daily between 1 and 2.30, by application to the Superintendent.

The North Terrace is open daily from 8 until sunset.

The Long Walk, with its avenue of elms, three miles in length, terminating at Snow Hill, with an equestrian statue of George III, by Westmacot; daily.

In the absence of the Court the public are also permitted to see the State Apartments, by free tickets, from the Lord Chamberlain (office in the Castle Yard), from 11 to 4 during April to October inclusive, as follows:–

The Queen's Audience Chamber
The Queen's Presence Chamber
The Guard Chamber
St George's Hall
The Grand Reception Room
Waterloo Chamber
The Grand Vestibule
The Grand Staircase
The State Ante-Room
The Queen's Drawing-Room
The Vandyke Room

The Round Tower may also be seen during the same hours as the State Apartments.

Windsor is connected with Eton by an iron girder-bridge, just below which the river divides; the right hand stream is the way to Romney Lock, the left one (*to be avoided in high water*) leads direct to the weir.

Eton College stands near the river, nearly opposite to Romney Lock, from which it is seen to advantage, but the entrance is at the bottom of the High Street, a short distance from the bridge. Eton College was founded by King Edward VI in 1440, and still continues to supply one-half of the scholarships to King's College, Cambridge, as well as some seventy students annually to the two chief Universities. The greater part of the College is of brick, and forms two quadrangles, the principal one having a picturesque clock-tower similar to Hampton Court, and a statue of the founder in the centre. The eastern side of this quad is taken up by the chapel, a fine stone building in the Perpendicular style; the interior of which contains a large organ, a beautiful screen between the chapel and ante-chapel, and amongst others two stained-glass windows to the memory of the Etonians who fell in the Crimean War. There are other buildings scattered round this large quad, and passing through the Cloisters we come to the playing-fields belonging to the College, situated along the bank of the river. At Eton College many of our celebrated men have received their education, among them being numbered the great Earl of Chatham, Horace Walpole, Fox, Wellington, Canning, Gray, Gladstone, etc.

Railway Stations – Windsor, SWR, in the Datchet Road, for Staines, Richmond, and London (Waterloo); GWR, High Street, branch to Slough, where the main line is joined for Paddington, Reading, etc.

Boats Housed and to be Let – G.F. Winter, Eton, R. Allen, Windsor side, H. Goodman, H. Parkins.

Hotels – The 'Bridge House', Eton side, The 'Christopher', Eton.

Inn – The 'Crown and Cushion', Eton.

There are other hotels in Windsor.

Fishing – Just below Boveney Weir, where the lock and weir streams meet, on the Bucks side of the river, there is capital bank-fishing for roach; and at Lower Hope, about mid-stream, many barbel are found. In Clewer mill-stream fine chub are taken; there is also excellent chub-fishing at the exit of the water at Dead Water Eyot; and from thence under the boughs down stream for a quarter of a mile quantities are caught, whipping with large artificial flies, either bees or palmers. A little above the GWR Bridge on the Windsor side is a capital gudgeon pitch. Good bank-fishing for roach is had from the Brocas shore; quantities are also captured at the back of the 'Fireworks Eyot', on which is the grand pyrotechnic display at the Eton festival on the 4 June; and barbel are nearly everywhere in the reach above the bridge.

Below Windsor Bridge some fine trout are always taken each season, and from Eton Weir to the playing-fields, for about half-a-mile, is a famous trout stream, in which some spotted beauties sport, and are often captured from the island. 'New Works Hole', opposite 'Sixth Form Bench', where the best cricketers of the school have tea on summer evenings, is a famous deep for barbel; while at 'The Needles', that 'meeting of the waters', where the different streams divided by Romney Island unite, is one of the choicest spots for punt-fishing on the entire Thames; it is much frequented by London anglers. The only other noticeable spot in the Windsor and Eton district is 'Hog Hole', about 300 yards above Victoria Bridge, in mid-stream; it is of great depth, and full of dace, chub, and barbel, with an occasional trout.

Fishing from the different weirs on the Thames is only allowed by a half-guinea yearly ticket issued by the Thames Conservancy, and the owner of the ticket is required to enter his name in the lock-keeper's book every time he uses the weir. Tickets can be obtained from the Secretary, Thames Conservancy, Trinity Square, Tower Hill, London.

Fishermen – R. Gray, Jas. Gray, J. Maisey, G. Plumridge, G. Hill, J. Bunce, W. Palmer, T. Bunce, J. Butler, S. Holland.
Fish – Trout, barbel, chub, roach, pike, gudgeon, perch, etc.
Fishing-tackle Maker – Bambridge, Eton.
Bathing – At Athens, on the main stream. Windsor Bathing place (by subscription), close to GWR, on Windsor side. Cuckoo Weir, a branch of the Thames opposite Clewer Point. Windsor Weir for Eton Masters and officers of the Guards.

ROMNEY LOCK from Windsor Bridge, *3 furlongs 96 yards; to Victoria Bridge, 6 furlongs 34 yards: falls from 2 ft 6 in in high to 7 ft in low water; average in summer, about 6 ft 3 in*

Below Eton we pass, for the first time, under the line of the South-Western Railway, which is carried over the river by an elegant girder-bridge. Just below the railway bridge stands Black Potts, the origin of which was a little fishing house, where the well-remembered Isaac Walton* used to angle for the finny tribe, in company with his friend, Sir Henry Wootten, then Provost of Eton.

Soon after, we arrive at the Victoria Bridge, the first of the twin viaducts which span the river at each end of the Home Park. These are stated to have been partly designed by the late Prince Albert, and the towing-path between them being claimed as Her Majesty's private property, no person is allowed to land except those in charge of barge-horses, or towing a boat.

The river at Victoria Bridge has a double curve-shaped deep channel; the remainder of the stream being shallow, persons in charge of boats drawing much water therefore require to be careful in their steering, or they may find themselves hard on. Near this bridge stood Herne's Oak, celebrated by Shakespeare, where:

> Herne the hunter,
> Some time a keeper here in Windsor Forest,
> Doth all the winter time at still midnight
> Walk round about an oak.

* Sir Isaac Walton (1593–1683) was the author of the famous book *The Compleat Angler or the Contemplative Man's Recreation* (1653). It includes practical information on angling, and scenes of rural life and folklore.

Henry Taunt on his houseboat c. 1885

It was said to have been blown down by a summer storm in August 1863.

Windsor Forest covered an enormous area in olden times. It comprised part of Berkshire, Buckinghamshire, and a considerable tract of land in Surrey, extending beyond Chertsey to Wycliffe's Oak, and to Hungerford, down the vale of Kennet. Even now the boundaries of the park, including the farms belonging, are extensive, reaching in one direction to Virginia Water, a distance of nearly six miles.

DATCHET

Station – (SWR) Windsor branch, about a furlong from the river.

A bridge formerly crossed the river at Datchet, which was removed when the Home Park was enclosed. Just above, at Hog's Hole, was the supposed scene of Falstaff's ducking out of the linen buck basket, when he exclaimed, in such feeling expressions, that 'the water swells a man'.*

Datchet was the resort of the 'Merrie Monarch',† who used sometimes to angle here, as has been told in some rather uncomplimentary verses, attributed to the Earl of Rochester:

> Methinks I see our mighty monarch stand,
> His pliant rod now trembling in his hand,
> Pleased with the sport – good man – nor does he know
> His easy sceptre bends and trembles so;
> But see, he now does up from Datchet come,
> Laden with spoils of slaughtered gudgeons home;
> Nor is he warned by their unhappy fate;
> But greedily he swallows every bait,
> A prey to every king-fisher of state.

Datchet is a pleasant little village, mostly clustered round a green, on one side of which stands the church, with a spirelet peeping over the other buildings. There is an old house or two, and also some modern half-timbered ones, that harmonise very happily with the green and its surroundings. About a mile from Datchet is Upton Church, an old Norman edifice, with centre 'ivy mantled tower', and close by, Upton Court, a fine specimen of a Jacobean timber-built house, standing on the site of an old monastery.

* *The Merry Wives of Windsor*, Act III, scene v.
† The title of 'Merrie Monarch' is associated here with Charles II.

Boats to Let – M. Cox, Jas. Hoare, J. Fenn, G. Keen.
Hotels – The 'Royal Stag', The 'Manor',
Fishermen – George Keen, J. Hoare, J. Hoare Jun., G. Lumsden.

From Datchet the river skirts the Home Park till it arrives at the Albert Bridge, the second of the twin viaducts before mentioned; just below which is Old Windsor Weir stretching entirely across the old river, and with a side overflow at the entrance to the cut which, leading to the lock, shortens the navigable part of the river more than a mile.

To avoid danger, hug the towing-path bank either in entering or leaving the cut.

Part of the old river is called Colnbrook Churchyard; the popular legend being, that in the beginning of the seventeenth century, when highwaymen infested the main London road from Hounslow Heath to Colnbrook, and Claude du Val* was the great captain of the band, the bodies of all travellers who lost their lives in the frequent deadly encounters were brought by night to this place in sacks heavily weighted and thrown into the Thames.

It is a fact that some time ago an entire skeleton, which had been evidently long embedded in the mud, was discovered here by some ballast heavers.

OLD WINDSOR LOCK from Albert Bridge *6 furlongs 214 yards; to Magna Charta Island, 1 mile 3 furlongs: falls from 3 ft in high to 6 ft 6 in in low water: average in summer, about 5 ft 6 in*

At Old Windsor Lock the fall of the river is used to drive the turbine supplying water to the Castle, etc., and just below the lock the main river is again joined. A quick stream leads us down to the bend; the river being shallow on the towing-path, land when fairly round the corner, and proceed, if wished, a short distance up the narrow lane to Old Windsor Church, with its lovely churchyard, the resting place of the fair Perdita.†

Old Windsor can boast of greater antiquity than its now greater neighbour-

---

* Claude Duval (1643–70) came from France and though a notorious highwayman is also remembered for his eccentric desire to teach English footpads to rob politely. He was hanged at Tyburn.

† The 'Fair Perdita' was Mrs Mary Robinson (1757–1800), author of poems and other literary works. Her grave has also been known as the 'Tomb of the Fair Shepherdess'.

hood, it being a royal residence of the Saxon monarchs, and as late as 1107 Henry I held his court in it, but there are no remains of the palace.

Hotel – 'The Bells of Ouzeley'.

Boats to Let – W. Haines and Son.

Fishermen – W. Haines and G. Haines.

Just below the 'Bells' the county of Berks is changed for Surrey. On the hill is Beaumont House, now a Catholic College and here the road turns off up to Cooper's Hill.

MAGNA CHARTA ISLAND from Old Windsor Lock *1 mile 3 furlongs; to Bell Weir Lock, 1 mile 3 furlongs 157 yards*

Following down the river we come to a broad meadow, the famous Runnymede, where, on the 19 June 1215, the barons were encamped, when they forced King John to meet them, and sign the celebrated Great Charter of England, which has made our liberties the envy and admiration of all other nations. The Charter was signed on the island on the farther side of the river, called, after this event, Magna Charta Island, well marked by the pretty stone cottage peeping out from amid the trees; in the hall the stone on which the Charter was said to be signed is preserved.

Below is Ankerwycke, with its pretty landing-place, called 'The Picnic', shaded by some grand limes, the house standing back some little distance from the river. The ruins of part of the old priory, founded by Sir Gilbert Montfitchet in the reign of Henry II, for Benedictine nuns, are still extant. Near them are several magnificent cedars, and an immense yew tree, said to have stood there when Magna Charta was signed. This is traditionally the meeting-place of Henry VIII with Anne Boleyn, and he is also stated to have waited here for the signal announcing her execution on Tower Hill. Cooper's Hill, which now rises before us on the opposite side of the river, has been immortalised by Denham* in his beautiful descriptive poem, of which the following is a specimen:

* Sir John Denham (1615–69) was born in Dublin and educated at Oxford. An ardent Royalist, he was forced to flee to the continent in 1648, but was appointed surveyor-general at the Restoration. Influential in the field of literature, his works include the famous topographical poem, *Cooper's Hill* (1642).

Ankerwycke, Wraysbury c. 1870

My eye, descending from this hill, surveys
Where Thames among the wanton valleys strays:
Thames – the most loved of all the ocean's sons
By his old sire – to his embraces runs,
Hasting to pay his tribute to the sea,
Like mortal life to meet eternity.

Godlike his unwearied bounty flows,
First loves to do, then loves the good he does.

O could I flow like thee, and make thy stream
My great example, as it is my theme!
Though deep, yet clear; though gentle, yet not dull;
Strong without rage, without o'erflowing full.

The view from the hill is very beautiful. Looking over a broad pleasant valley, Windsor Castle can be seen rising up like an island in a sea of verdure; and the scene is bounded beyond by the range of the Chilterns, with their varied contour stretching across the field of view. The summit is occupied by the Royal Engineers' College; and in the distance is the little town and church of Egham, the new Holloway College for the higher education of women, being on the lower part of the hill.

The river below Ankerwycke makes a sharp double curve, then a reach of uninteresting character past the varnish works, and Bell weir and lock are reached. Keep close to the towing-path bank in high water to avoid the weir. *Fishing* – Close to the 'Bells' is a good place for gudgeon, where they are to be found in large quantities; and from here right down below Ankerwycke is first-class water for trolling and roach-fishing. Barbel find a home close to Magna Charta Island, and also at the Bell Weir; whilst under the boughs on the Buckinghamshire side perch and chub are to be found.

EGHAM

BELL WEIR LOCK Egham, from Magna Charta Island, *1 mile 3 furlongs 157 yards; to Staines Bridge, 7 furlongs 195 yards: falls from 1 ft in high to 6 ft in low water; average in summer, about 5 ft*

Railway Station – Egham (SWR, Reading branch), about 5 furlongs from the river.

Egham village mostly consists of one long street built on both sides of the London road. The church is a grey brick building with stone dressings, and

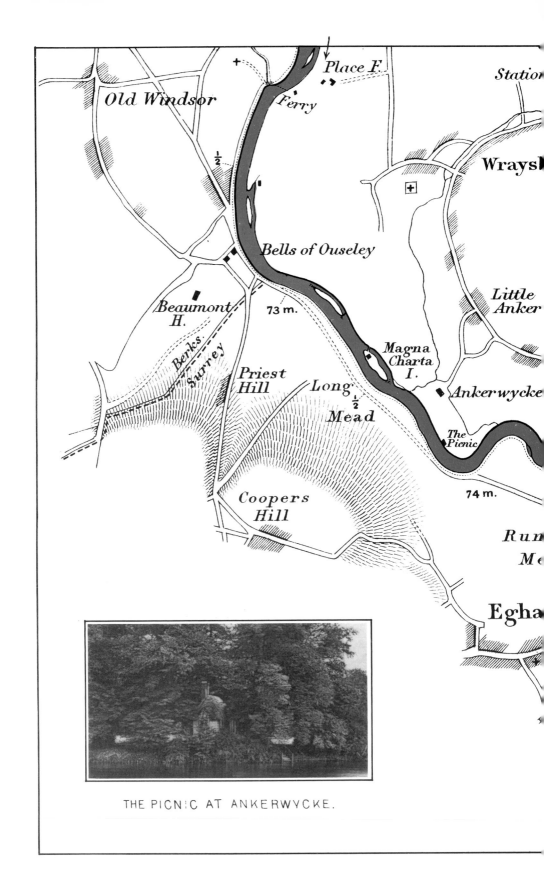

Old Windsor

Place F.

Station

Ferry

Wraysb

½

Bells of Ouseley

Little
Anker

Beaumont
H.

73 m.

Magna
Charta
I.

Ankerwycke

Berks.

Surrey

Priest
Hill

Long
½
Mead

The
Picnic

Coopers
Hill

74 m.

Run
Me

Egha

THE PICNIC AT ANKERWYCKE.

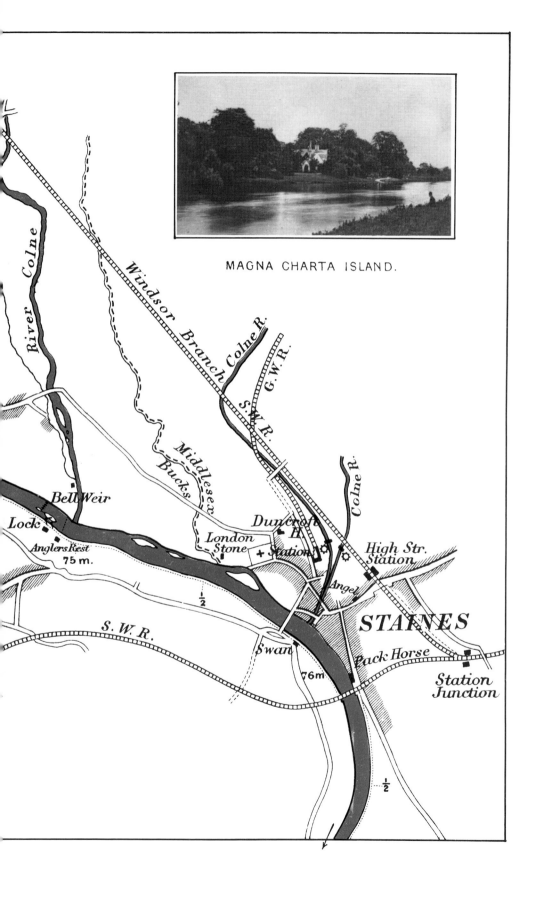

MAGNA CHARTA ISLAND.

River Colne

Windsor Branch

Colne R.

G.W.R.

S.W.R.

Middlesex

Bucks

Bell Weir

Lock

Anglers Rest
75 m.

Duncroft
H.

London
Stone

+ Station

High Str.
Station

Colne R.

Angel

½

S. W. R.

STAINES

Swan

76m.

Pack Horse

Station
Junction

½

small tower completing the western façade. It contains a curious monument to Sir John Denham, and also to his two wives.

Hotel – 'The Catherine Wheel'.

Inn – at Bell Weir, 'The Anglers' Rest'.

Boats Let and Housed – 'Anglers' Rest'.

Just below Bell Weir Lock a ferry crosses to Wraysbury or Wyardisbury, and the main stream of the River Colne runs into the Thames. This stream, which is interesting from its connection with Milton, rises near Hatfield, Hertfordshire, and uniting with several other streams flows past St Albans, Watford, and Rickmansworth, to Chalfont, Uxbridge, and Colnbrook, soon after dividing into several branches, which all flow into the river here or at Staines.

STAINES

STAINES BRIDGE from Bell Weir Lock *7 furlongs 195 yards; to Penton Hook Lock, 1 mile 6 furlongs 168 yards*

At the boundary stands London Stone, a landmark which has existed for several centuries, which not only marks the division between the counties, but also the limit of the ancient jurisdiction of the City of London on the Thames.

Round the top of the original stone is the inscription, 'God preserve the City of London, AD 1280'; the greater part of it being still legible – and it is here that the swan markers belonging to the London Companies, when making their annual journey up the river marking the swans, bump their new hands, and in that orthodox way make them ever afterwards free of the river.

Staines Church stands at a little distance behind London Stone; it is a brick edifice, with square western tower. A new apse has lately been added to the chancel.

Near the church is an old house called Dun Croft, stated to be the site of a palace of King John. It has a very picturesque old front of the time of James I, with Oriel windows and ornamental chimneys, a centre porch, with ivy mantling up each side, and heavy mullioned windows. The south side of the house is of later date, the porch being of the style of Queen Anne's reign. The interior also possesses some interesting features.

Staines Bridge is of white granite, built by Rennie, after two or three failures to erect a substantial structure a little below. It was opened in state by King William and Queen Adelaide in 1832.

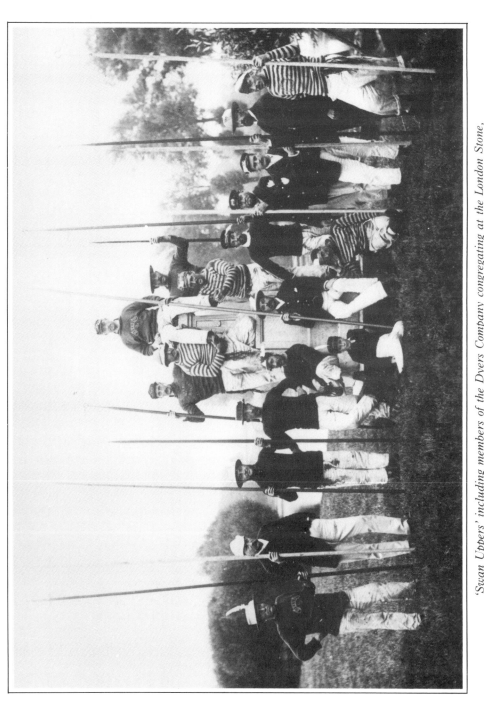

'Swan Uppers' including members of the Dyers Company congregating at the London Stone, Staines, c. 1883

Staines is a quiet little town, very clean and bright; but its general trade seems to a certain extent crippled by its near proximity to London. It has lately made an advance in erecting a new Town Hall and public buildings, which are a credit to the place. It also boasts a large brewery, and the original manufactory of Linoleum, a kind of floor-cloth made partly from cork.

Stations – SWR Junction, Waterloo, Windsor, and Reading; also SWR, High Street (Windsor branch), both about 3 furlongs from the river. GWR, branch to Colnbrook and West Drayton, Moor Lane.

Post Office, lower end of the High Street, open on week days from 7 a.m. till 8.30 p.m., and Sundays from 7 a.m. till 10 a.m.; the last post for London being at 8.35 p.m.

Boats to be Let and Housed – J. Tims, near the church and below the Railway Bridge; E. Burgoyne at the Railway Bridge; A.S. Wallis, at the 'Packhorse'.

Hotels – The 'Packhorse', close to the river, The 'Angel', The 'Swan'.

Fishing – At Staines Bridge there is excellent barbel fishing, and from the bank close by; just below, where the drain from the Brewery enters is roach and gudgeon fishing. In the back-water perch are to be found, and above London Stone, a fly will generally secure a fine chub. At Bell Weir Lock are some excellent swims. Below Staines Bridge is a good roach swim, and a little farther down, close to where the old bridge used to stand, is a noted swim for barbel. Along the towing-path, still farther on, is very respectable bank-fishing, whilst at Truss Island are perch and roach.

Fishermen – Thomas Fletcher; J. Keen, J. Keen, Jun., H.J. Clark.

Bathing – Tims' Bathing-house, near the church.

Just as we leave Staines we pass under the iron girder-bridge of the SWR branch to Reading; and here begins the broader towing-path which stretches along that part of the river over which the City had jurisdiction.

LALEHAM

PENTON HOOK LOCK from Staines Bridge *1 mile 6 furlongs 168 yards; to Laleham Ferry, 6 furlongs 140 yards: falls 2 ft; does not vary much*

Penton, or Penty-hook, as it is often called by the country people and fishermen, is the first of the 'City Locks' we come to, having been built by the Conservators of the Thames when the conservancy of this part of the river was

STAINES CHURCH.

STAINES BRIDGE.

CHERTSEY LOCK & BRIDGE.

SCALE 2 INCHES TO A MILE.

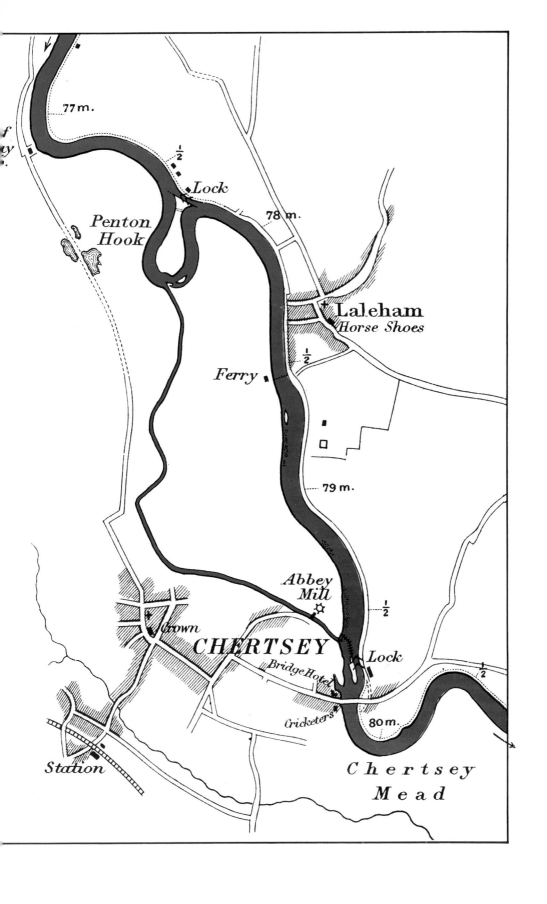

vested in the Lord Mayor and Corporation of the City of London. The City Locks include Penton Hook, Chertsey, Shepperton, Sunbury, Moulsey, and Teddington, and in olden times were free to pleasure traffic; they were all built since 1815. The river at Penton Hook makes a curious bend or hook of a little less than a mile in length, returning nearly to the same spot, the lock cut being made just across the neck of the hook. From the further side a brook leaves the main river, which was made by the monks of Chertsey Abbey to supply themselves with water-power to turn their mill, and it still is utilized for that purpose.

Below Penton Hook is the very pleasant village of Laleham, only a small portion of which is seen from the river. The church is partly an ancient structure, but has been at some time maltreated in an abominable manner, and requires thorough restoration. The river spreads itself out very wide at the Ferry, and in places shallows considerably, and this compels boats towing here to use an extra long towing-line, if they wish to get along freely. Laleham Ferry with its weeping willows makes a pretty bit, and from it a path leads to Chertsey Town.

Inn – The 'Horseshoes'.

Boats Let – F. Trotter, at Ferry, W Harris.

Fishing – The river round Laleham has long been a noted fishing locality, and in past times it was perhaps the best spot on the river for fly-fishing, etc. Strange to say, dace which once were so plentiful here, are comparatively scarce, and barbel and roach seem to have taken their place in the catches.

Trout are to be found round the Hook, and at Laleham, and there are also some dace still along the shallows. The overfall at Penton Hook is entirely removed, and that specially favourite spot for fishermen is no longer what it once was, when the water rushed over in graceful ripples, and formed many an eddy in which fish used to play and feed.

Fishermen – Wm. Harris, Alfred Harris, G. Harris, Arthur Harris, E. Harris.

Below Laleham the scenery is flat; the river on the Surrey side is bordered by a number of rushy islets, amongst which the white water-lily, the queen of Thames flowers, grows in great numbers. These beautiful flowers are now so fashionable, that in some places they are fairly dying out, and in a few years will be extinct, if dragged up in the ruthless way they often are. A long mile brings us to Chertsey Weir, to avoid danger from which, when the weir is open, *keep close to the towing-path*.

CHERTSEY

CHERTSEY LOCK from Laleham Ferry *1 mile 1 furlong 4 yards; to Shepperton Lock, 1 mile 7 furlongs 183 yards: falls from 8 in in high to 3 ft 9 in in low water; average in summer, 3 ft 6 in*

Chertsey lock-house stands in Surrey, although on the Middlesex side of the river. Traces are still in existence of the curved channel in which the Thames here ran, but on the lock being built the course of the stream was altered as at present.

Up to the backwater, beyond the weir, the river is joined by the Abbey Mill stream; the old mill, a picturesque wooden structure, with its quaint outbuildings, being the successor of that built by the monks.

Chertsey Bridge, built in 1785, at a cost of £13,000, is a stone bridge of seven arches, with the roadway rising to a pitch similar to Richmond Bridge.

Chertsey town is nearly half a mile from the bridge, and although an old place retains few marks of its antiquity. Its church is comparatively modern, and has few interesting features. Its ancient importance was entirely derived from its abbey, which was founded as early as the year 666, for Benedictine monks. Between this and the ninth century no record seems to exist; but at that date we read of the monastery being destroyed by the Danes, who sailed up the Thames in their ships, devastating the country all round; and not content with plunder, they murdered the abbot, one priest, and all the monks, ninety in number. Edgar, in 964, rebuilt and refounded the monastery; and, in conjunction with Ethelwold, ejected the monks already there, and replaced them by others willing to submit to a stricter rule. This building seems not to have lasted long, as in the *Saxon Chronicle*, dated 1010, it is recorded that, 'this year men began to work at the new monastery at Chertsey.' The monastery prospered after this. It is said to have covered four acres of ground, and looked like a town. The abbot wore the mitre, and was also a temporal baron, owing military service to the king. In the reign of Henry II the Abbot of Chertsey, with other abbots, priors, and bishops, was summoned and attended the king at Berwick-on-Tweed with military retainers, horses, and arms, to join an expedition against the Scots.

It was to Chertsey, in 1471, that the body of the unfortunate King Henry VI was brought for interment from Tower Hill. After being carried through

CHERTSEY
BRIDGE ✳ HOTEL.

SPENCER & SARGENT   PROPRIETORS

The Hostelry has recently undergone a thorough renovation, with an enlargement
of the premises and erection of first-class STABLES and BOAT HOUSES.

ANGLERS AND ROWING MEN
will find the best of Accommodation with Moderate Charges.

Large Dining Saloon,
admirably adapted for Society Dinners, Wedding Breakfasts, and Masonic Banquets.

PRIVATE SITTING ROOMS and BEDROOMS en suite.

FIRST CLASS CUISINE.

THE HOTEL AND LAWN
is surrounded with some Charming Scenery.

Head Quarters of
THE ALBION SOCIAL CLUB, CHERTSEY ROWING CLUB, and
CHERTSEY ANGLING ASSOCIATION.

Flys sent to meet Trains.

the streets to Blackfriars, the body, 'without a coffin, was put on board a boat, and rowed up the river to Chertsey Abbey,' and there 'consigned to mother earth without priest or clerk, torch or taper, singing or saying,' as an old recorder states; but other accounts differ as to this. A few years after the body was removed to Windsor, and buried in St George's Chapel. The abbey was finally dissolved in 1536, in the reign of Henry VIII, at which time the clear income amounted to £659 15s. 8¾d., the gross revenue being considerably more. The destruction of the building is thoroughly complete – not a vestige left, except a fragment of wall, a rude gateway, a small part of a farmhouse, and the stream which still works the picturesque timber-built mill.

Chertsey is also known from its connection with Cowley the poet,* who, becoming disgusted from his not receiving the office he had been promised, retired to this quiet town, where he died from a fever. The house he occupied (in Guildford Street) once had a projecting porch; this has been removed to add to the width of the street; but a tablet was affixed to the house, which still remains, on which is the following line:

Here the last accents flowed from Cowley's tongue.

St Anne's Hill, near Chertsey, was the seat of Charles James Fox, the celebrated politician, during the stormier part of his public career; and here he gladly exchanged party warfare for the enjoyment of rural life and occupations.

Chertsey Station – Branch, SWR, at the bottom of Guildford Street, more than a mile from the bridge.

Hotels – The 'Chertsey Bridge'. Landing stage just above the bridge, The 'Crown', in Chertsey.

Inn – The 'Cricketers'.

Steam Launch and Torpedo Builder – C. Des Vignes.

Steam Launches to Let – James Taylor.

Boats to Let – Tom Taylor and Son; and at the 'Chertsey Bridge' Hotel.

Fishing – Chertsey Weir Pool is said to contain nearly every kind of Thames fish: barbel, bream, perch, trout, carp, and jack are taken there. Above the

---

* Abraham Cowley (1618–67). Educated at Cambridge, he was a writer and poet who contributed to the Royalist cause in both England and France. His works include *The Puritan and the Papist* (1643); *The Mistress* (1647) and *The Visitations and Prophecies concerning England* (1660–61). The latter years of his life were spent in retirement at Barnes and Chertsey.

WEYBRIDGE.

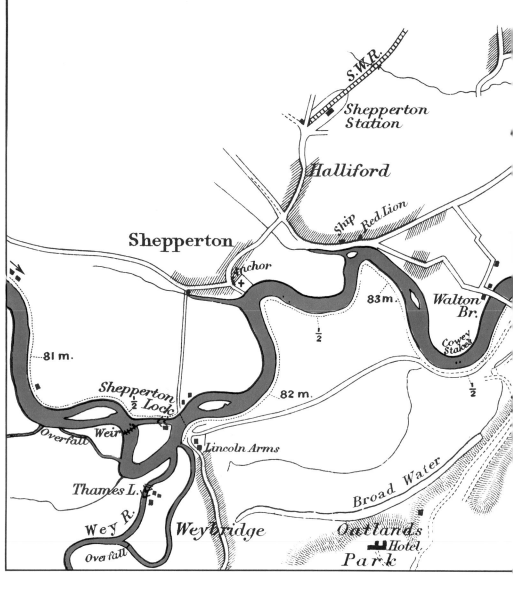

Sunbury

White Horse

Magpie

Lock
½

Fish
Ponds

Weir Hotel
Sunbury Weir
85 m.

Water
Works

86 m.

½

erfall

½

Walton
+ on Thames

ley
k

AT WALTON.

SUNBURY.

lock, chub, barbel, roach, and jack are to be found by the little rushy islets, and below the bridge are trout, while dace and roach abound in places.
Fishermen – W. Galloway Sen., J. Haslet, J. Poulter, T. Taylor Sen., T. Taylor Jun., H. Purss, L. Hackett.
Bathing – Below the weir.

WEYBRIDGE

SHEPPERTON LOCK from Chertsey Lock *1 mile 7 furlongs 183 yards; to Halliford Point, 1 mile 2 furlongs 33 yards: falls from 2 ft in high to 5 ft 9 in in low water; average in summer, 5 ft 3 in*

Above Shepperton Lock the river receives the stream from Virginia Water, which waters Chertsey in its course, and below the weir the Bourne brook, rising near Cobham, also falls into the Thames. Shepperton Lock is situated on a short cut, the main river making a detour through the weir, and twisting round again to the bottom of the lock, where is also the horse ferry. The main river receives here the waters of the River Wey, which, rising in Hampshire, is made navigable from Godalming, a distance of some twenty miles, and is joined above New Haw Bridge by the Basingstoke Canal.

The Wey joins the Thames by two mouths, the upper being the navigable one; at the mouth of the lower branch will be found the 'Lincoln Arms' hotel, for many years kept by the well-known fisherman, J. Harris. This river, in parts, is rather picturesque, and a few miles up, passes the ruins of Newark Abbey, with its legend of the monks who 'built a tunnel under the Wey'.

Weybridge lies mostly a little way from the river. It is a long straggling place, with some traces of old-fashioned picturesqueness about it, which are rapidly transforming themselves into a brand-new look; villa residences have been springing up on every hand, but the old green fortunately has up to the present escaped. A monument which once did duty elsewhere, stands on the green; and the church, a beautiful modern edifice with a high broach spire, is seen a little way beyond. The bridge over the Wey, from which the name of the place is derived, is an iron girder structure, substantial and by no means in bad taste; it carries the Chertsey road over the river. Not far from Weybridge is Oatlands Park, with its once celebrated grotto (which still exists). This was at one time a royal domain, being *exchanged* by Henry VIII for some other manor, and was occasionally the residence of Queen Elizabeth. It was of vast extent, but has been considerably cut up by villa residences, etc., into a number of parts. A modern hotel has been built near the site of the mansion, useless to river tourists, and of which little can be said for its management.

Weybridge Station – SWR, about a mile from the river.

Hotel – The 'Lincoln Arms'.

Boats to Let or Housed – W. Harris, 'Lincoln Arms', S. Nicholls, Weybridge, D. Hackett, Shepperton Lock.

Fishing – The reach from Chertsey Bridge to Shepperton is a very fine one for all kinds of fish; Chertsey Scour is good for trout and dace; Dumsey Swim being a fine place for barbel and dace, and Datchet Point for pike. At the back of Shepperton Weir, down to the landing for Weybridge (the whole of the back-water leading up to the weir), is one of the finest streams for trout we have about here, and in the Weir Pool are barbel, trout, perch, and roach.

Fishermen – J. Upsdal, 'Lincoln Arms', T. Poulter, A. Poulter, H. Curr.

Bathing – In the back-water below the weir.

UPPER SHEPPERTON

Station – Shepperton (SWR, Thames Valley branch), a short mile from the village.

Shepperton Church peeps over the other buildings at the angle of the river, and forms the centrepiece to a pretty bit of landscape. It is a plain Gothic building, with western brick tower of later date.

Shepperton, like Weybridge, is a well-known spot for anglers, and here is one of the deeps which many anglers well know. These 'deeps' are spaces of the river of two or three hundred yards in extent, granted by the Corporation of the City of London to the several towns and villages on the river from Staines to Richmond.

A deep thus given is appropriated and preserved expressly for angling, no net or engine of any sort being allowed to be used in it. The fishing on the river is far better looked after than in years gone by. Fish are only allowed to be taken over a certain size; in nearly every important place is a local society for preserving the waters, and besides this there are a number of river keepers, appointed by the Conservancy Board and the Thames Angling Preservation Society, to look after and stop anything like netting or unlawful fishing. At all the fishing places, as indeed now at nearly every place on the river, will be found fishermen who make it their business to prepare the ground and supply punt, etc., for the day's fishing; and as far as possible we have taken every care to give a correct list of these men at each place.

Hotel – The 'Anchor'.

Boats to be Let or Housed – G. Purdue.

Fishermen – Wm. Rogerson, F. Purdue, G. Rosewell, H. Purdue Jun., W. House, J. Haslet.

HALLIFORD, OR LOWER SHEPPERTON

HALLIFORD POINT from Shepperton Lock *1 mile 2 furlongs 33 yards; to Walton Bridge, 6 furlongs 156 yards*

Station – Shepperton (SWR), a short mile from the river.

Halliford is really a part of Shepperton, advantage being taken of the bend in the river. It is a very pleasant stopping place, the hills of Oatlands Park and Walton forming the background to the views of the river. Like Shepperton and Weybridge it is a favourite angling quarter, and the same class of fish are to be met with.

At the bend below Halliford, where the river curves towards Walton Bridges, is the traditional spot called Cowey Stakes, where Caesar is said to have crossed the river by a ford, to invade the Kingdom of Cassivelaunus. The river was supposed to have been fortified with pointed stakes driven into its bed, and some few years ago stakes were recovered from the stream in this spot, which bore all the signs of great age. Close by is an intake of one of the London Water Companies.

Hotels – The 'Red Lion', the 'Ship'.

Fishermen – Ed. Rosewell, T. Purdue, Wm. Rosewell, Edwin Rosewell, H. Rosewell.

WALTON-ON-THAMES

WALTON BRIDGE from Halliford Point *6 furlongs 156 yards; to Sunbury Lock, 1 mile 5 furlongs 130 yards*

Station – Walton (SWR), about 1½ miles from the river.

Walton is a double bridge, or, strictly speaking, two bridges, the one over the river and the other over a tract of marshy land. The bridge over the river is an iron girder structure, that replaced an older bridge, part of which fell down.

Walton is a small country town, lying a little back from the river. Its church is an ancient structure erected in the twelfth century, with nave, two aisles, and curious old flint tower at the western end. It contains, amongst others, a sculptured monument to the memory of Lord Shannon, by the celebrated Roubillac. A large black marble tablet also, to the memory of William Lily, astrologer to King Charles I, was placed in the church by his friend Elias Ashmole. In addition to these is a curious brass, on which is engraved the figure of a man riding on a stag, into whose neck he is plunging a sword. This person (Selwyn) is said to have leapt on the back of a stag in the heat of the chase; to have guided it with his sword towards Queen Elizabeth, and when he came near her plunged it into the animal's throat, so that it fell dead at her feet. In the vestry is preserved a scold's gag, or gossip's bridle, as it was called. The bridle enclosed the head, and was fastened behind with a padlock: a small piece of iron being so placed as to press down the tongue of the offender. Thus compelled to be silent, 'she was led round the town by an officer to her shame and punishment,' and this was continued until she began to show signs of promise to amend.

Hotels – 'Anglers', 'Swan'.

Boats to Let or Housed – S. Rosewell, E. Clark and Sons.

Fishing – At Walton is one of the best pitches for bream on the Thames, not far from the old wooden bridge that carries the towing-path over the entrance to the backwater; and, in places all the way to Sunbury Weir, bream and barbel are to be found. Chub likewise and dace exist along the Middlesex shore, whilst now and then trout make their appearance. Roach fishing, however, is better than any other, and is mostly practised by the fishing visitors.

Fishermen – G. Hone, S. Rosewell, J. Hone, R. Watford.

Sunbury Lock c. 1880

SUNBURY

SUNBURY LOCK from Walton Bridge, *1 mile 5 furlongs 30 yards; to Hampton Ferry, 2 miles 0 furlongs 110 yards: average fall, 6 ft. Boat-launch just above the lock*

Station – Sunbury (SWR), Thames Valley branch, about 1¼ miles from the river.

After leaving Walton our attention is attracted by a building with a lofty chimney, standing a little back from the river, which is another of the waterworks which supply London with filtered water from the Thames; and then comes Sunbury Weir, with the river surging over it, and creating the pleasing variety of sound which falling water always makes. Be cautious in high-water times to keep near the towing-path, as the draught of the weir is very strong, and has caused more than one accident.

Sunbury Weir was rebuilt in 1885 on a new plan, with double iron sluices, the bottom one of which is raised first. It directly faces the stream, but on the side of the river furthest from the towing-path, the remainder forming an overfall over which the water rushes in the most picturesque way.

Close by the lock are the interesting ponds for breeding Thames trout and other fish; and the river-keeper will be pleased to explain their peculiarities.

Hotels – The 'Weir', Surrey side of the Cut, The 'Magpie', on the main river.
Boats to be Let or Housed – E. Clark and Sons, T. and A. Stroud.
Ponies for Towing – E. Clark and Sons.
Fishing – Sunbury Weir, with the stream running from it, is a fine reach for fly fishing, as well as for pike, barbel, and perch, with a few trout. The back-water, called Cane Edge, running behind the islands below the lock, is good for dace, while lower down, on the Middlesex shore, are chub and jack.
Fishermen – E. Clark and Sons, T. and A. Stroud.

Below the lock commences Sunbury Race, a sharp stream which flows for the next mile; in high-water time it is often pleasanter to take to the back-water, down which the stream runs more slowly. Passing the intake of the Lambeth Waterworks on the other side is the Grand Junction Waterworks, and passing Plat's Island a whole series of waterworks rear their towers on the Middlesex shore, while the church and village of Hampton completes the scene.

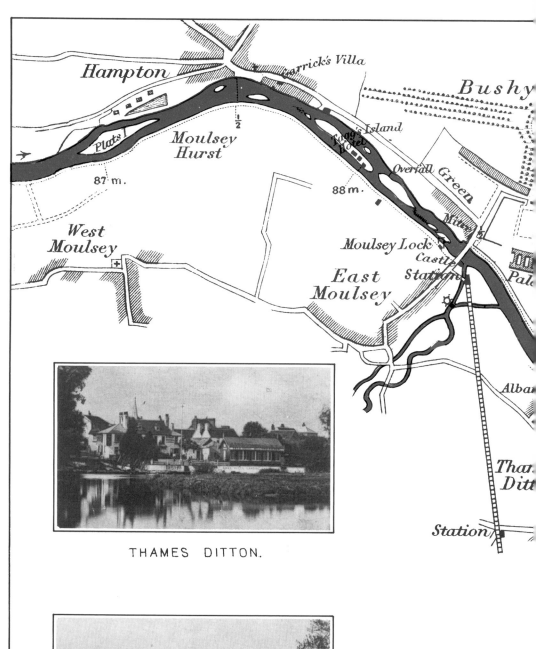

Hampton

Garrick's Villa

Bushy

Moulsey
Hurst

Plats

½

Fogg's Island

Overfall Green

87 m.

88 m.

West
Moulsey

Moulsey Lock

Castle
Station

East
Moulsey

Pala

Alba

Tha
Ditt

Station

THAMES DITTON.

HAMPTON COURT PALACE.

⅛   ¼   ½   1 m.

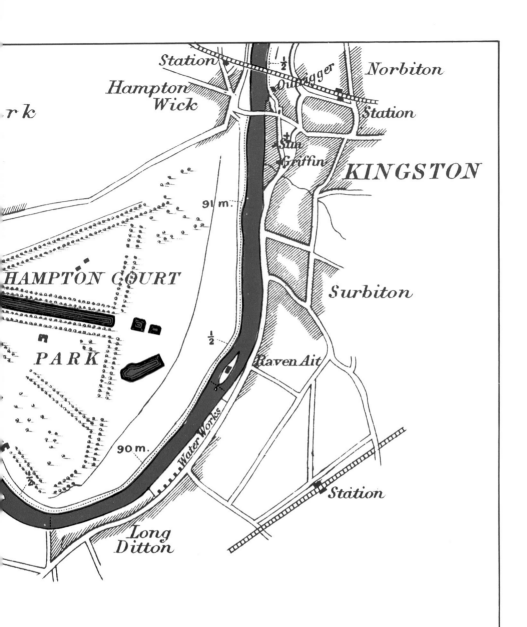

Station
Hampton
Wick

r k

½
Outrigger
Norbiton

Station

Sun
Griffin

KINGSTON

91 m.

HAMPTON COURT

Surbiton

PARK

½

Raven Ait

Water Works

90 m.

Station

Long
Ditton

CORONATION STONE_KINGSTON.

Hampton. The rotunda in the grounds of Garrick's villa, the home of the actor David Garrick c. 1883

HAMPTON

HAMPTON FERRY from Sunbury, *2 miles 0 furlong 110 yards; to Moulsey Lock, 6 furlongs 110 yards*

Railway Station – (SWR branch), about 1 mile from the river.

Hampton Church is a plain Gothic building, white brick and stone dressings with a western tower, standing close to the river, and is better seen from the side of the island just below the ferry. On the towing-path side is Moulsey Hurst, now a race-course; but once it had a more unenviable reputation, when prize fights took place, and even before that, when duels were the rage; but fortunately these are the disgraces of a bygone time. Below the church stands Garrick's Villa, the house in which the eminent actor David Garrick* lived after his retirement from the stage. It is well marked by the rotunda near it, close to the river, which contained the celebrated statue of Shakespeare, by Roubillac, now in the hall of the British Museum.

Here 'all the world' used to come in order to do homage to his ability, and listen to his lively conversation; a curious feature in the social history of England in the eighteenth century.

Hotels – 'Bell' and 'Red Lion'.

Boats to be Let or Housed – C. Constable, Benn and Son, J. Langshaw and Son.

Fishermen – Benn and Son, J. Langshaw and Son.

TAGG'S ISLAND AND HOTEL

Tagg's Island has been made into a first-class place for landing, picnic parties, and fishermen; the fishing all round the island is strictly preserved for angling. The origin of this place was a wooden hut on the rear of the island, dignified by the name of the 'Anglers' Retreat', which, with tea gardens and a skittle

---

* David Garrick (1717–79) one of the most celebrated actors in the history of the theatre. He is also remembered for his writing of farces, prologues and epilogues. From 1747 he was involved in the management of Drury Lane, where he produced many of Shakespeare's works.

alley, were fairly patronised, but after the experience of a flood or two, its then proprietor (one Harvey) deemed it judicious to seek drier quarters, and removed to the site of the present hotel.

Hotel – 'Island Hotel'.

Boats and Steam Yachts Built, Let and Housed – Island Boat House.

Fisherman – T. Wheeler.

MOULSEY AND HAMPTON COURT

MOULSEY LOCK from Hampton Ferry *6 furlongs 110 yards; to Thames Ditton, 1 mile 0 furlong 209 yards: falls on the average about 6 ft*

There is a boat-launch here, open in summer for small boats, to save them going through the lock. It consists of two double series of rollers down an incline, and is on the weir-side of the lock.

Hampton Court Station – SWR branch, close to the Bridge, Surrey side.

Hampton Court Bridge, just below the Lock, is rather a picturesque iron structure of five arches, erected 1865–6, at a cost of £11,176 which stands in the place of an old wooden bridge built in 1753, and connects the village of Moulsey with that of Hampton Court. Just below Hampton Court station:

> The soft windings of the silent Mole

finish; this river – rising on the borders of Surrey and Sussex, and flowing through some exquisite scenery – empties itself by two mouths:

> Close by those meads, for ever crowned with flowers
> Where Thames with pride surveys his rising towers,
> There stands a structure of majestic fame,
> That from the neighb'ring Hampton takes its name.

Hampton Court Palace stands on the Middlesex shore, the grounds reaching down to the towing-path, with terraces over-looking the river. At first sight it appears to be built entirely of brick, with stone dressings, and to consist of a long plain range of buildings, but this idea entirely disappears as we examine it more closely.

THE THAMES OF HENRY TAUNT

The history of Hampton Manor seems to date from the Doomsday Survey, when it belonged to Walter de St Waleric, and the whole value was £39. Early in the thirteenth century it was bequeathed to the Knights of St John of Jerusalem, in whose possession it remained till Wolsey induced the Prior of the Order to grant him a lease of it, and the building of the palace was begun in 1515. The stately style in which it was built, and the lavishness of its fittings, added to the gorgeous Court held there by Wolsey, excited the envy and anger of the King. Wolsey therefore presented it, with all its sumptuous furniture, to Henry, who in return 'licensed him to lie in his Manor of Richmond'; and taking possession of Hampton, enlarged the palace, and also converted the country round into a chase, which he stocked with deer. Edward VI was born here; his mother, Queen Jane Seymour, dying with his birth.

It was the occasional residence of the sovereigns in succeeding reigns, James I holding a 'Conference' here, and Charles I adorned it considerably with works of art. It was after used as his prison, and it was from here he attempted to escape, which ill-advised action led to his more rigorous confinement at Carisbrook. The Commonwealth saw the pictures dispersed, and the building itself, with the manor, sold for the sum of £10,700; but the latter deed was retracted, and Cromwell utilized the palace for his own residence. In 1690, under William III, a great part of the old palace was pulled down and rebuilt in its present form, under the direction of Sir Christopher Wren, the gardens being laid out after the French fashion by the two most distinguished gardeners of the day, London and Wise. The present arrangement of the park was partly made by William, and it was there that his death was caused through his horse stumbling over a mole-hill. Queen Anne here held her Court, which Pope, in his *Rape of the Lock*, has immortalised, giving us a sharply-drawn picture of the manners of that time. George II was the last monarch who resided here; and the private apartments are now appropriated for members of noble families; the remainder of the palace and gardens being thrown open for the gratification of the public. The State apartments are open every weekday, except Fridays and Christmas Day, from 10 a.m. till 6 p.m. in summer; on Sunday the palace opens at 2 o'clock.

Entering from the gate near the bridge, which is ornamented with the lion, unicorn, and other heraldic emblems, the first feature is a large open space partly shaded with grand elms: on the one side being a row of buildings forming the barracks.

The front makes an open quad, in the centre being the entrance tower, reminding one forcibly of Eton College. Underneath the archway is a fine fan-tracery ceiling, and this leads into the first Quadrangle or Court, which is 167 ft by 162 ft, and is part of the original palace of Wolsey. Facing, and surmounted by a clock, is another archway; and entering this turn to the right, and ascend the broad staircase to the Great Hall. This hall, one of the most striking features of the whole palace, was designed by Wolsey, but not commenced to be built for some five years after he had given up Hampton Court to Henry. It has the same general effect as Christ Church Hall, Oxford (also built by Wolsey), its dimensions being: length 106 ft, breadth 40 ft, height 60 ft (Christ Church Hall being: length 114 ft, breadth 40 ft, height 50 ft); but its greater height gives it an effect of airiness wanting in Christ Church. Note the roof with the beautiful hanging pendants repeated in Christ Church Hall, and also the Cathedral, Oxford. The walls are lined with tapestry, representing incidents in the life of Abraham. Eight pieces only are here, out of the series of ten. At the upper end of the hall is a beautiful bay with fan-tracery ceiling, and also the dais, on which the high table (where the most distinguished guests sat) was placed.

Tradition has it that in this very hall the drama of *Wolsey's Fall* was reproduced by Shakespeare before Queen Elizabeth. A doorway from the upper end of the hall leads into the withdrawing room, lined also with tapestry like the hall. Over the chimney-piece is a portrait of Wolsey, let into the panel, and on the opposite site of the room a large nearly semicircular bay projects into the kitchen court. Retracing your steps through the hall, and down the staircase, note that the ceiling of this gateway is covered with fan-tracery like the other tower, and leads into the second court. This quad is nearly 134 ft square, one side being occupied by the hall. Over the gateway at which you have entered is a curious astronomical clock, lately restored. A passage from this court leads to the chapel, open only for service on Sundays at 11 a.m. and 3.30 p.m. Along the southern part of this quad extends an Ionic colonnade by Sir Christopher Wren, and crossing to the end of this the foot of the King's staircase is reached.

You have now left the old part of the palace, and have arrived at that portion built some two centuries later.

Here leave impedimenta (if you have any, in the shape of umbrellas, parasols, sticks, or parcels of any description), in the care of the attendants, and ascend the staircase.

The ceiling and walls were painted by Verrio, a Neapolitan brought over by Charles II; and, although many of his details are condemned, the general effect of this staircase is gorgeous in the extreme, and captivates the eye at once. The staircase leads into the Guard Chamber, which is the first of the

State apartments, and this is followed by room after room, all having their lofty walls covered with splendid treasures of art.

It would be impossible in the limits of this work to give a complete guide to these, but at the King's staircase you will be able to procure one at 6*d*. or 1*s*. The range of apartments ends at the Queen's staircase, from whence we pass into the cloisters, which surround the Fountain Court. And here the difference in style is painfully apparent in the huge staring white sashes and bars of the windows, the straight crossing lines of which tire the eye to a great extent. This is part of Wren's palace, and contains the apartments last visited. A few steps through another gateway leads out to the gardens and park, the beauty of which at once takes away the feelings of pain which the last court gave.

The beds in autumn are often laid out in a carpet-like pattern, and may be considered slightly stiff; but to those who love nature wild, this is well recompensed by the Wilderness, which is entered by a gateway a little north of the palace. Here nature has been allowed to paint her own pictures in her own way, and right royally has she done so; these ten acres of pleasant paths, under the shade of the grand old trees, may well be termed 'a place for whispering lovers made'. At the farther side of the Wilderness is the Maze, which is the cause of more fun than any other part of the grounds, and ought not to be missed, the joke of continually taking the wrong path and finding yourself brought to a dead stop is so provokingly amusing that, if you have a fit of the 'blues', try a 'dose' of the maze. After finding your way out again, pass through the Lion Gates and cross over the road into Bushy Park, where, in the season, the beautiful avenues of chestnut trees are covered with their glorious flowers, presenting a scene unequalled elsewhere. Then, after a peep at the bronze fountain of Diana, double back through the Lion Gates to the palace again. The private gardens, as they are called, are all open to the public; and beautiful terraces stretch down to the Thames, from which a fine view of the garden-front of the palace is seen. The Vinery, with its wealth of Black Hamboro' grapes, had better not be visited if you are at all inclined to covet, as the 2,500 bunches of grapes are not grown for river tourists, but reserved for Her Majesty. Before leaving the palace do not forget to call for the articles you left with the attendant at the King's staircase.

Among the favourite pastimes of the London people who visit Hampton Court is a trip on the river; and oarsmen with every kind of style, good, bad, and no style at all, are to be seen enjoying their holiday.

Boats to be Let and Housed – Harry Tagg, Moulsey, close above the bridge, C. Whatford, Hampton Court, W.T. Abnett, Hampton Court, R. Tagg, J. Williams and J. Tribe.

Hampton Court Bridge with Harry Tagg's 'Thames Boat Building Works' and landing stage in the foreground c. 1878

Hotels – 'The Castle', Moulsey, 'Mitre', Hampton Court; 'Prince of Wales', Moulsey.

Fishing – Moulsey Weir is noted for its trout and barbel, and good fishing is to be had at Hampton Court Bridge, just below. The water gallery hole, close under the rails on the towing-path side, is also a safe refuge for good trout; and on the other bank the shallow water will repay a cast with the fly. Roach, dace, and gudgeon abound all down this reach; and in some places heavy perch are to be found. The overfall on the back stream at Moulsey Weir at one time in the spring is a remarkable sight, from the enormous quantity of dace and other fish rushing up the tumbling bay, in their efforts to reach the upper water, where they go to deposit their spawn.

Fishermen – Wm. Milbourne, T. Davis, T. Whatford, T. Wheeler, J. Smith, G. Martin, T. Milbourne, J. Hedger, C. David, J. Williams.

THAMES DITTON

From Hampton Court the river is very pleasant, with its fringe of trees skirting the bank; but the earth hunger we Britishers are accused of by our American friends is beginning to line the shore opposite Hampton Court; and the entirely rural charms of the river at ''Appy 'Ampton' will some day be a thing of the past. The island also, which used to be just below Hampton Court, has entirely disappeared. It was partly ballasted and partly washed away, but a shoal is left which is better avoided in short-water time.

Thames Ditton is prettily situated, partly behind the islands, with the odd spire of the church peeping over the trees.

Theodore Hook immortalised it in some verses long ago, the memory of which is still preserved in the village, the following lines being a good specimen of the ode:

> When sultry suns and dusty streets
> Proclaim town's winter season,
> And rural scenes and cool retreats
> Sound something like high treason
> I steal away to shades serene
> Which yet no bard has hit on,
> And change the bustling, heartless scene
> For quietude and Ditton.

THE THAMES OF HENRY TAUNT

The mighty Queen whom Cydnus bore,
  In gold and purple floated,
But happier I, when near this shore,
  Although more humbly boated.
Give me a punt, a rod, a line,
  A snug arm chair to sit on,
Some well-iced punch, and weather fine,
  And let me fish at Ditton.

Here Lawyers safe from legal toils,
  And Peers released from duty,
Enjoy at once kind Nature's smiles,
  And eke the smiles of beauty;
Beauty with talent brightly graced,
  Whose name must not be written,
The Idol of the fane is placed
  Within the groves at Ditton.

Here in a placid waking dream
  I'm free from worldly troubles;
Calm as the rippling silver stream
  That in the sunshine bubbles:
And when some Eden's blissful bowers
  Some abler bard has writ on,
Despairing to transcend his powers,
  I'll *ditto* say for *Ditton*.

The church consists of a nave and chancel, with a number of aisles on both sides, making the whole edifice as broad as it is long. The western tower is flint-built, like the greater part of the church, and is capped with a picturesque wooden structure, out of which springs the little spirelet which peeps over the houses in the scene from the river. There are some engineering and bronze casting works behind the island.

Railway Station – SWR, about 4 furlongs from the river.

Hotels – The 'Swan', The 'Albany'.

Boats Housed and to be Let – R. Whatford, E. and A. Tagg, H. Rogerson, C. and W. Tagg.

Ferries – Queen's Ferry, just below Hampton Court; Ditton Ferry, from the 'Swan' landing.

Fishing – There are trout in the river here, but they are not often caught. Barbel are plentiful, and roach, dace, and gudgeon are nearly everywhere down the whole of the reach to Kingston. At Thames Ditton deeps are jack; along the walls of the waterworks below are heavy perch; and a good place for a variety of fish is the mouth of the Surbiton sewer, where nearly every day

may be seen more than one punt with fishermen landing their finny prey.
Fishermen – H. Rogerson, E. and A. Tagg, C. Tagg, W. Tagg.

At Long Ditton boats are let by H. Hammerton and Sons and J.H. Buttery and Son; the latter of whom also pursues the occupation of fisherman. The left bank of the river still winds round the outskirts of Hampton Court Park, the right being occupied by the immense filter beds, etc., of the Waterworks at Seething Wells until Raven Ait is reached.

SURBITON

Surbiton (corrupted from South Barton) is a very pleasant modern suburb of Kingston, stretching some distance along the river, the bank of which is utilized and forms a very agreeable promenade called 'Kingston Parade'. Villa residences line the road and form side streets and crescents, the railway station (SWR main line) being about 3 furlongs from the river.

The reach to Kingston is the course over which the Thames Sailing Club hold their races, and at the end of the parade is Surbiton Catholic Church, looking out from between the trees.
Boats Let and Housed – Raven Ait Boat Co., P. Parker.

KINGSTON

KINGSTON BRIDGE from Thames Ditton, *1 mile 7 furlongs 55 yards; to Teddington Lock, 1 mile 6 furlongs 88 yards*

Kingston Railway Station and Hampton Wick Station – SWR, both about 3 furlongs from the bridge.

Kingston Bridge is a graceful white stone structure, with five elliptical river arches and several land arches, opened in 1828. It was built at a cost of £40,000, and replaced one of the oldest wooden bridges on the river. Kingston is worth a visit, and the whole of the sights being in and near the Market Place, little time need be wasted in seeing them.

The church dates from the reign of Richard II, but parts have been added and rebuilt, and lately the whole south aisle has undergone restoration. Its brick tower forms a bold object from the river.

The Market Place is a fine open space with the Town Hall in the centre, in

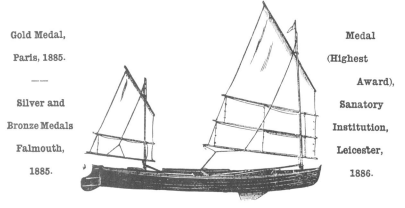

front of which stands a statue of Queen Anne; and close by is a graceful new monument to the memory of H. Shrubsole, Esq., thrice mayor of the town. At the lower end stands the Coronation stone of the Saxon Kings of England, who were crowned upon it when 'Cyningestane' was the Royal town where these ceremonies were performed, and a list of names of some eight or nine Saxon monarchs is placed round it.

The great pride of Kingston is its history. From the earliest it has been a place of importance, and there is some show of probability that the Romans had a station here. In Saxon times it was a royal town, its name Cyningestane being given to it from its possessing the King's Stone of the Saxon kings. The banquet at the coronation of Edwy in 955 took place at Kingston, and was followed by the events which led to the brutal branding and horrible murder of the unfortunate Queen Elfgiva, and the deposition and death of the king. The Domesday Book mentions Kingston as a royal demesne, but its first charter it owes to John. In 1264 Henry III took and demolished the castle, which was held by the Earl of Gloucester for the barons.

Sir Thomas Wyatt, when marching to London during his revolt against Mary, after the execution of Lady Jane Grey, crossed the Thames at Kingston. The bridge had been broken through by command of the council, but was repaired and utilized by Wyatt's followers. In the civil war Kingston was held for the king; and it was here that the last effort was made to revive the royal cause. When Charles was a prisoner in the Isle of Wight, and the royal troops everywhere disbanded, the Earl of Holland, with the Duke of Buckingham, collecting about 600 men, made this their headquarters, and issued addresses to the citizens of London, calling upon them to rise and rescue their Sovereign. Parliament, as soon as it heard of the rising, sent some troops of horse from Windsor, who defeated the Royalists on Surbiton Common, and ended the attempt.

Kingston was in olden times a 'right merrie' place; as the following quotations show:

1570. Paid to ye ryngers when ye Earle of Northumberland was taken, twenty pence.
1581. For rynginge when ye traitors were taken, ninepence. For rynginge when Don Pedro came through ye towne, two and sixpence.
1624. To ye ryngers for joy of ye Prince's return, three and fourpence.

And the following very curious entry:

Paid for a year's whipping of ye dogges out of ye church, eightpence.

STAR & GARTER _ RICHMOND.

View from E.E.L. PIE ISLAND.

TEDDINGTON LOCKS.

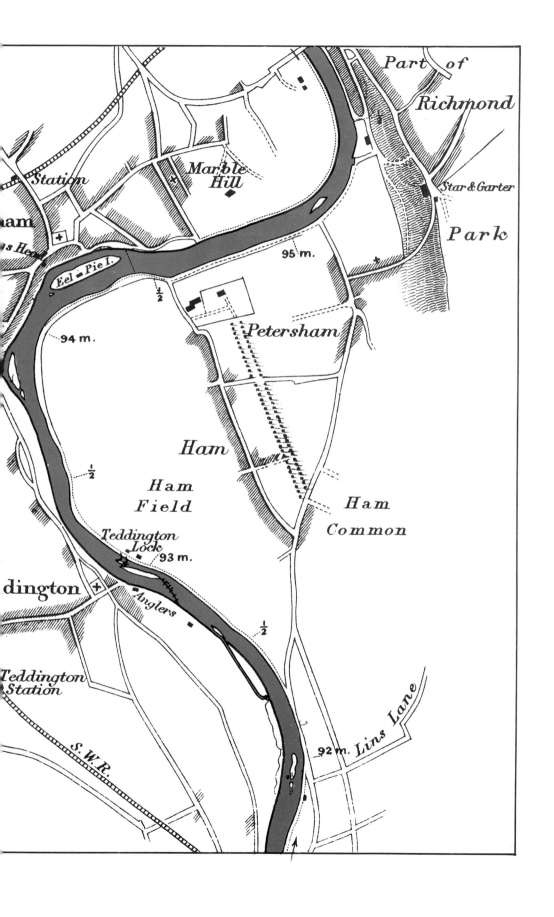

At Teddington, the Angler's Hotel and A.F. Pocock's boathouse c. 1883

A large market is held in the town, and it is also the headquarters of several leading rowing clubs.

A short distance below Kingston Bridge the SWR crosses the river over one of their characteristic iron girder bridges.

Boats Housed and to be Let – R.J. Turk, C. and A. Burgoine, Kingston and Hampton Wick, F. Eastland, B. Pope.

Hotel – The 'Sun'.

Fishing – At Kingston, fishing is fully up to the average for roach, chub, and bream; barbel are to be found near both the bridges; and below the railway bridge, close to the mouth of the sewer, are roach, with splendid barbel in a hole close by; chub line the aits below, where a fly may be thrown with every chance of success; and fine jack abound all along the reach down to Teddington Weir, just above which, at Rat Island, is a good place for roach and perch.

Fishermen – J. Johnson Senr., Wm. Clark, J. Johnson Junr., W. Wilks.

Swimming baths above the bridge, and below at the islands.

TEDDINGTON

TEDDINGTON LOCK from Kingston Bridge *1 mile 6 furlongs 88 yards; to Eel-Pie Island, 1 mile 1 furlong 22 yards: falls from 6 in at high tides to 5 ft 9 in in low summer water; average in summer, about 5 ft*

Railway Station – SWR, 5 furlongs from the river.

There is a large boat slide here with three sets of rollers, and also a small side-lock for pleasure boats, both situated a little above the main lock. Tide flows one hour.

Teddington Lock and Weir are the last on the Thames; the latter is a fine, nearly new weir, partly constructed of iron, very different from the old wooden structure which preceded it. The flow of the tide usually ends here, and by some authorities is stated to be the cause of its designation, from Tide-end-town, but now and then the rise is sufficiently high to force back the river as far as Kingston, or even further, fairly turning the weir the reverse way. This happened on the morning tide of 28 October 1882, and several other tides in that year were nearly as high. Teddington Lock is the largest on the Thames, but will not compare with some of the locks on the Severn for either size or height. The village lies on the further side of the backwater, and extends mostly up one road to the railway station and Upper Teddington. Like all places near London it has grown enormously within the last few years, and whole rows of shops and brand-new villas have sprung into existence in many directions. It is in contemplation to throw a footbridge across the lock cut and main stream to the village, and part of the money has been collected, the design being a suspension bridge of a very graceful character. A footbridge is sadly needed as the watermen here demand the extortionate sum of three pence as their fee from passengers crossing the ferry: and give as a reason the fact (?) that being *below* Teddington Weir they are under the control of the Watermen's Company, and that their rules *allow* them; but even if this be so it does not diminish the imposition of the case.

Teddington Church is fairly picturesque, more from the position it occupies than the edifice itself. It stands only a short distance from the river.

Among the notable residents of Teddington were the Earl of Leicester, the favourite of Elizabeth; Penn the Quaker, who from here wrote his defence when his complicity with James had brought upon him the accusation of being himself a Papist; and Paul Whitehead the poet. The latter is buried in the church, with the exception of his heart, which was removed to West Wycombe, and deposited in the mausoleum belonging to his patron, the Lord Despencer, with an appropriate rite. 'Pretty Peg Woffington'* is another of the Teddington notables; she lies in the churchyard.

Boats Housed and to be Let – T.A. Pocock, R.H. Porter, Simmons and Sons.

Hotel – The 'Anglers', close to the river.

Watermen – E. Cripps, W. Simms, J. Lewis, R. Hammerton.

Ferry – across the backwater.

Fishing – The fishing below Teddington, and also at the Weir, is thoroughly good, as is well attested by the numerous fishing-punts that ever and anon dot the river down to Richmond Bridge. The favourite spots are the Weir pool, where barbel exist in full force; and just at the bend of the river above Twickenham, where often as many as twenty punts are moored in close contact, the occupiers fishing for dace and roach. Lampreys are caught early in the year at Teddington Weir, but not in such numbers as formerly. At low tide also one of the favourite methods is wading in the stream and taking dace with the fly, this mode often resulting in a heavy take.

Fishermen – J. Baldwin, C. Baldwin, B. Stevens, F. Kemp, E. Cripps.

Between Teddington and Twickenham are the well-known mansions of

---

* Margaret Woffington (1720–60), a famous actress.

Strawberry Hill and Pope's Villa. Strawberry Hill lies back from the river, and derives its fame from Horace Walpole* (afterwards Earl of Orford), the author of *The Castle or Otranto*, who amused himself for many years in enlarging and beautifying it; rebuilding the greater portion in a kind of toy-Gothic style, and filling it with every conceivable kind of nic-nac and curiosity. A smaller place below *Great* Strawberry Hill is Little Strawberry Hill:

> Here lived the laughter-loving dame,
> A matchless actress, – Clive her name:
> The comic muse with her retired,
> And shed a tear when she expired.

So wrote Walpole on the urn he erected to her memory.

Pope's Villa† stood just below where the curve of the river round to Twickenham begins. It was pulled down by Lady Howe, and the willow also perished which was so well known as being planted by the poet. The house has been replaced by a Chinese pagoda style of building, which is easily recognised in passing; and the grotto still exists, but in a mutilated state.

Pope's residence here has immortalised this spot; and both from his letters and poems we learn the history of his pursuits and hopes in connection with his grotto, in which he took a great delight, and for which he wrote the following lines:

> Nymph of the grot, these sacred springs I keep,
> And to the murmur of these waters sleep:
> Ah! spare my slumbers, gently tread the cave,
> And drink in silence, or in silence lave.

He lies buried in Twickenham Church.

---

* Horace Walpole (1717–97) was the fourth son of Sir Robert Walpole, and was himself an MP and writer. He settled in Twickenham in 1747 where he created Strawberry Hill, his 'Little Gothic Castle'.
† Alexander Pope (1688–1744). The son of a linen draper of London, he was largely self educated. His early life was spent at Binfield in Windsor Forest. Famous for many poetic and literary works including *The Rape of the Lock* (1712) he moved to Twickenham in 1718 where he devoted much of his time to his garden and grotto, as he became increasingly interested in landscape gardening and the 'cult of the picturesque'.

Twickenham. The 'chinese style' house built on the site of Pope's villa c. 1878

TWICKENHAM

EEL-PIE ISLAND from Teddington Lock, *1 mile 1 furlong 22 yards; to Richmond Bridge, 1 mile 4 furlongs 140 yards. Tide flows, 1½ hours*

Railway Station – SWR, junction for Staines, Kingston, Shepperton, etc., about 3 furlongs from the river.

The old village of Twickenham lies on the Middlesex shore, partly in the backwater behind Eel-Pie Island, which latter won its name from its connection with a favourite luxury of our forefathers, now virtually extinct on the river.

The church is not a beautiful piece of architecture, with the exception of the ancient and time-worn tower; and is only interesting from containing the tomb of Pope. Sir Geoffrey Kneller, the artist, also lived in the village.

Hotels – 'Eel-Pie Island', 'Albany'.

Boats to be Let – Cooper, J. Coxon, C. Shore.

Watermen – G. Lee, C. Lee, J. Jones, J. Ricks, T. Lee, Walter Hammerton, William Hammerton, A. Hammerton, M. Hammerton, H. Hammerton, and R. Hammerton.

Fishermen – S. Cole, E. Finch, T. Coxon, J. Coxon, T. Chamberlain, J. Brand, S. Mesley, W. Francis, R. Moffatt, J. Hennessey, G. Chamberlain, P. Hammerton, W. Spong, J. Dobbin, and H. Spiers.

Just below Eel-Pie is Twickenham Ferry, and then follows Orleans House (known by the vases of flowers on the river wall), for some time the residence of the Princes of Orleans, now the headquarters of the Orleans Club. The octagon room was built for the purpose of entertaining Caroline, Queen of George II, at dinner, by Mr Secretary Johnstone, the then owner of the mansion.

Nearly opposite, on the other bank of the river, is Ham House, a curious and almost perfect mansion of the time of Charles II, nearly hidden by trees. This was the birthplace of the celebrated John, Duke of Argyle, and was also the place to which James II was ordered to retire on the arrival of the Prince of Orange in London, but not deeming himself safe he fled precipitately to France. This reach of the river is very beautiful when full of water, but at low tide the dirty mud banks with which it is lined sadly mar its loveliness; and the shallows which then abound, with the swift stream, take away much of the pleasure which would be felt were this part of the river locked as the reaches above. The Thames Conservancy have spent and are still spending money in dredging this reach, but in spite of all they have done the river is but little improved. Marble Hill is the next notable mansion, built by George II for the Countess of Suffolk, the Earl of Pembroke being the architect, and the gardens laid out by Pope. The village of Petersham now peeps between the trees on the towing-path bank, but this is scarcely noticed, as before us lies the grand panorama of Richmond.

RICHMOND

RICHMOND BRIDGE from Eel-Pie Island *1 mile 4 furlongs 140 yards; to Kew Bridge, 2 miles 7 furlongs 124 yards; tide flows, 2 hours*

Railway Station – L & SWR and North London line; both stations being close together, about 3 furlongs from the bridge.

Richmond received its name by royal command from Henry VII, its original name being Schene (shining). It was, like Kingston, a royal town, the Palace on the Green being a favourite residence with some of our kings and queens. Henry I had a house here, and several of his documents are dated from Schene. Edwards I and II also resided here, and Edward III, after a long and victorious reign, died here in 1377, deserted by all his friends, even the dearest of them flying from his side, and leaving him to die without attendance.

Richard II resided here during the earlier part of his reign; and Chaucer, the first of English bards, was Surveyor of Works to the Palace of Sheen, under this monarch. Anne, the consort of the king, died in the palace, and Richard was so grieved that he cursed the building and refused to inhabit it. It was the favourite residence of Henry VII, who rebuilt the palace after its destruction by fire, and changed its name to Richmond; and here many of his most sumptuous entertainments were given. Henry died here in 1509. Henry VIII also resided here in the earlier years of his reign; but Wolsey's Hampton Court so completely eclipsed Richmond and excited his envy, that Wolsey found it necessary to propitiate him by presenting him with that palace, which then became the royal habitation. In return the King licensed Wolsey 'to lie in the manor of Richmond'; but when the common people saw, they remarked,

'See a butcher's dog lie in the manor of Richmond!' This did not last long, for Wolsey's disgrace and death happened soon after. Queen Elizabeth was a prisoner here during part of the reign of her sister Mary; and she also inhabited it as queen, and died here in 1603. According to local tradition, the room over the gateway is that in which the Countess of Nottingham died, after the interview with Elizabeth, in which she confessed to having kept back the ring which Essex, then under sentence of death, had entrusted her to deliver to the Queen. In the time of the Commonwealth the palace was dismantled, and from that time has gone to decay. A very small trace now exists, on the western side of Richmond Green, consisting of a gateway and turreted building. The Green was once the favourite jousting place, in the balmy days of the palace, and is still used as a recreation ground.

The old church has few architectural beauties, but contains a medallion to the memory of Edmund Kean, the actor, and a brass with inscription above the last resting place of Thomson the poet, whose beautiful poems of the *Seasons*, the *Castle of Indolence*, etc., have passed into standard works.

But all the interest arising from these historical recollections is eclipsed by the natural beauties which unfold themselves as we pass towards the Hill. At its foot nestles the Duke of Buccleuch's house, amid all its wealth of grand old trees, whilst the centrepiece of the whole scene is the palatial building of the far-famed 'Star and Garter', with its terraces and walks on the brow of the hill. The prospect will well repay the climb to the top, the boat in the meanwhile being left in charge of any of the watermen at Petersham corner, or at the bridge. The view from the hill has been one of the chief favourites with many of our English landscape painters, being one of the loveliest on the river – little being wanting: wood and water, softly-swelling hills and hazy distance, with village spires and lordly halls, are blended in beautiful harmony. From the hill a vast expanse of country stretches far away, till the distance is closed by the hills of Buckinghamshire on the one hand, and the Surrey Downs on the other. A grand description of this loveliness is portrayed in Sir Walter Scott's *Heart of Midlothian*; the poet Thomson also, and Malet, have both described it in glowing language, but not more so than its exquisite beauty deserves.

From the Hill pay a visit to the Park, at the entrance of which the 'Star and Garter' stands. This park, eight miles in circumference, and containing 2,253 acres, was enclosed by Charles I, to the great annoyance of some of the owners of the land. The right of a free passage through the park was tried by an action-at-law at Kingston assizes, brought against the Princess Amelia by John Lewis, a brewer of Richmond, and decided in favour of the people's right, although every effort was employed by the crown to stop the right of way.

View at MORTLAKE.

RICHMOND BRIDGE.

View from RICHMOND HILL.

SCALE 2 INCHES TO A MILE.

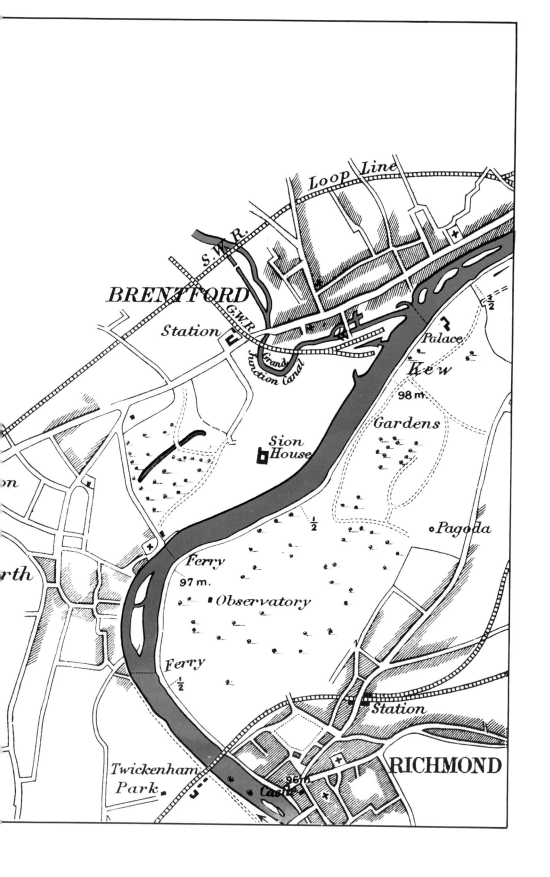

Back to the river, the bridge is the next notable object. It is a fine stone structure of five arches; and, being picturesquely situated with the little islands below it, is an ornament to the river. The first stone of the bridge was laid on 23 August 1774. It was opened in 1777.

The post office is in George Street, three minutes' walk from the bridge, and open on week days from 7 a.m. till 9.30 p.m., the last post for London being at 10 p.m.

Boats Housed and Let – E. Messum and Sons, Chas Wheeler, F. Thompson, J. Ellsley, J. Glover, J. Callis, Chitty and Peasley, C. Brown, E. Redknap, H. Redknap.

Watermen – C. Wheeler (in ordinary to the Queen), W. Platt, G. Platt, J. Mansell, R. Chitty, E. Chitty, A. Chitty, J. Mackinny, J. Whitfield, J. Cox, T. Mackinny, E. Mackinny, J. Peasley.

Hotels – 'Star and Garter', 'Talbot', 'White Cross'.

Fishing – The fishing round Richmond is often very good, the takes being mostly dace and roach. Barbel are also found in some places, and eels at certain states of the tide.

Fishermen – H. Mansell, C. Brown, G. Howard, H. Howard, G. Platt, H. Wheeler, J. Brain, W. Platt.

ISLEWORTH AND SION

Below Richmond is the Old or Little Park, on part of which once stood the priory of Sheen, one of the religious houses in which Mary reinstated the dispersed monks; and here also stood Sir William Temple's house, where Swift* resided with him. William III used to visit here, and it was at Sheen that Swift met Stella, whose story forms so sad a chapter in his biography. She was the daughter of Sir William Temple's steward.

It was designed to construct at these islands a lower lock than Teddington, which, if done, would make the Richmond and Twickenham reach one of the finest on the river; but engineers are divided in opinion as to the practicability of the work, and thus it has fallen through. We hope that some future engineer will devise a way for the accomplishment of this scheme; such an improvement would be the fund of an immense amount of pleasure to Londoners and

---

* Jonathan Swift (1667–1745) was the cousin of the poet Dryden and secretary to Sir William Temple. His *Journal to Stella* (Ester Johnson) was written in 1710–13.

the residents of this neighbourhood. The same thing has been done success-fully elsewhere; at Gloucester, for instance, where the tides rise much more fiercely than on the easy flowing Thames.

Isleworth was once called Thistleworth, as we learn from surveys prior to 1769. It is partly situated behind the islands. Below them stands the church, the body of which is of brick, with no architectural beauty; the tower, built in 1706, partly ivy-covered, being more picturesque. Sion, just below, the princely seat of the Duke of Northumberland, was originally a monastery for the order of St Bridget, the only one of the kind in England. It was one of the first religious houses suppressed by Henry VIII, and at that time its revenue amounted to no less than £1,944 11s. 5¼d. per annum. Sion was retained by the King, and served as the prison of his unhappy wife Katherine Howard till her execution, and it was here than his own corpse rested on the way to Windsor. Edward VI presented it to the Protector Somerset, and after his attainder and execution to the Duke of Northumberland. Lady Jane Grey resided here when offered the crown, the accepting of which led to her death and that of the Duke, when the estate once more reverted to the Crown, and was restored by Mary to the 'Sisters of all the Saints, and especially St Bridget'. Elizabeth dispossessed them, and gave Sion into the hands of the Duke of Northumberland, in whose family it still remains.

Boats Let or Housed – J. Waite, W. Styles.

Inns – 'Northumberland', 'London Apprentice'.

Ferry – To Kew Gardens below the Aits.

BRENTFORD

'Tedious town. For dirty streets and white-legged chickens known' sings one of our poets; like all pushing, busy places (even the docks and business-places of London), it is untidy sometimes; and its factories in some parts are rather annoying to the olfactory sense; still it is not so bad as we might imagine at first sight.

Brentford is a quaint old town, mostly one long street on the London Road. It still contains some very picturesque old houses with overhanging bay windows on the first floor. Brentford Old Parish Church has been taken down and rebuilt. St Lawrence, near the bridge, has few attractions beyond its western tower, but St Paul's, a more modern church, has a fine western tower and spire.

Brentford takes its name from the little River Brent, the bridge over which, in the reign of Edward I and afterwards, was kept in repair by a toll on every Jew and Jewess that passed over it. In 1016, Edmund Ironsides defeated the Danes here, and drove them out of London, compelling them to take to their ships, and afterwards – crossing the ford over the river – he fought against the army and put them to flight. In 1642 the Battle of Brentford was fought, and the Parliamentarians were defeated by Prince Rupert, who aimed to seize the artillery lying at Hammersmith; but in this he was unsuccessful, and retired on the arrival of Essex with the main army.

The Grand Junction Canal ends here; it begins at Branston, in Northamptonshire, and covers a distance of about ninety miles, with the average of a lock per mile. The toll for pleasure boats is 21s., steam launches, 40s. The dock here is often very animated when a large number of boats are waiting for the tide to flow, and, although in their cups sometimes bargemen are quarrelsome, yet ordinarily they are quite as good-natured and obliging as the majority of the working classes.

Brentford Bridge, like Staines and Kew, has a dire penalty attached to anyone injuring it, which the following copy of an iron tablet on it shows:

NOTICE – MIDDLESEX TO WRIT.
Any person wilfully injuring any part of this county bridge will be guilty of FELONY, and upon conviction be liable to be kept in PENAL SERVITUDE FOR LIFE.
7 & 8 Geo. 4, c. 30. 2s. 19. By the Court. SELBY. 1825.

Brentford Railway Station – GWR is just beyond the bridge.
Boats Let or Housed at the Ferry – J. Bridgman.
Inn – The 'Bunch of Grapes'.
Ferry – To Kew Gardens.

KEW AND STRAND-ON-THE-GREEN

KEW BRIDGE from Richmond Bridge *2 miles 7 furlongs 124 yards; to Barnes Railway Bridge, 2 miles 0 furlong 178 yards. Tide flows, 3 hours*

Kew Railway Stations – SWR, and North London, nearly close to the bridge. Middlesex side.

Steamboats – Run from Kew Bridge Pier to all piers to London every forty minutes.

Kew Bridge resembles Richmond Bridge, and like it is substantially built of stone. It is from the design of Payne, and was erected in 1790.

Kew Green is a few yards from the south end of the bridge, and is ornamented by the church, which stands on one side of it. The latter contains the tombs of Gainsborough and Zoffany, the celebrated artists. The main entrance to Kew Gardens also opens on the Green, but there are other entrances close to Isleworth Lower and Brentford Ferries.

Kew Gardens, which border the river on the Surrey shore, are a great attraction, and well worthy of a visit, if time can be spared. They were *private* pleasure grounds belonging to the Crown, but during the reign of Her present Majesty they have been put under the management of the Commissioners of Woods and Forests, as public national gardens, and in their style they are unequalled. Kew Gardens open at 12 noon, the houses and museums at 1 p.m. on week days, and continue open until dusk. On Sundays they open at 1 p.m. The principal entrance on Kew Green is through the ornamental iron gates which open on to a broad walk. To see the gardens quickly turn to the left, the following being the most notable parts, but complete guides are to be obtained at the entrance gates.

The Fern Houses; the Victoria Regia House; the Rock Garden; No. 2 Museum; No. 1 Museum; the Lily House; the Palm House; the Temperate House; and finish with the 'North' Gallery, which latter is a grand collection of paintings of flowers in many parts of the globe, the work of one lady named North, who has spent years in their production. This should in no case be missed. Glance also at the Pagoda down the vista of trees (163 ft high), and note the flagstaff (159 ft high) as you come back. You will thus get an idea of the houses and grounds, but the whole of a day can well be spent there.

The old Palace of Kew stands between the grounds and the river. It is a red brick Elizabethan building and faces the Palm House. The Palace is not open, but the gardens and houses are all open and free.

Strand-on-the-Green, below Kew Bridge, has no noticeable features; but was the residence of Joe Miller,* whose jests are even still often passed off as original happy thoughts.

---

* Joseph or Josiah Miller (1684–1738). Commonly called Joe Miller, he was an actor and reputed humorist. His reputation was retained after his death by the publication of a collection of his jests *Joe Miller's Jests* (1739).

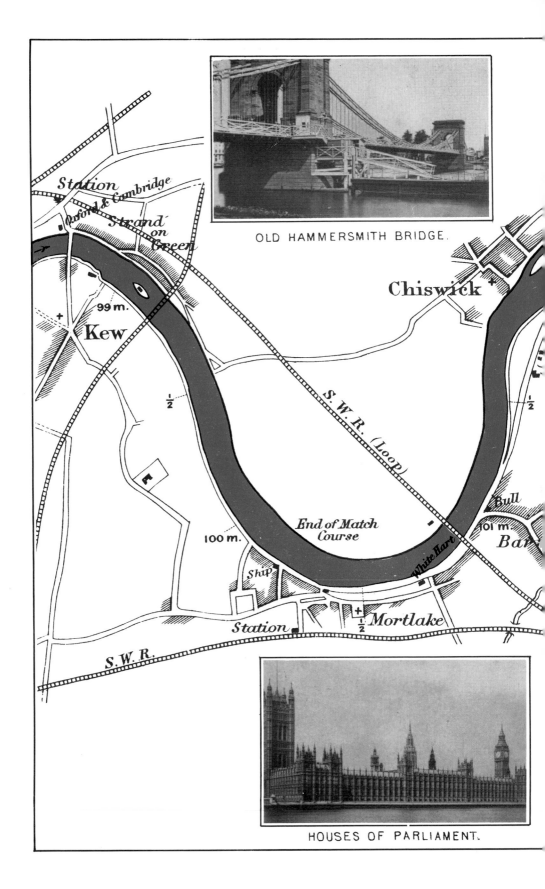

OLD HAMMERSMITH BRIDGE.

Station

Oxford & Cambridge

Strand
on
Green

Chiswick

99 m.

Kew

½

S. W. R. (Loop)

½

Bull

100 m.

End of Match
Course

White Hart

101 m.

Bar

Ship

Station

+ ½

Mortlake

S. W. R.

HOUSES OF PARLIAMENT.

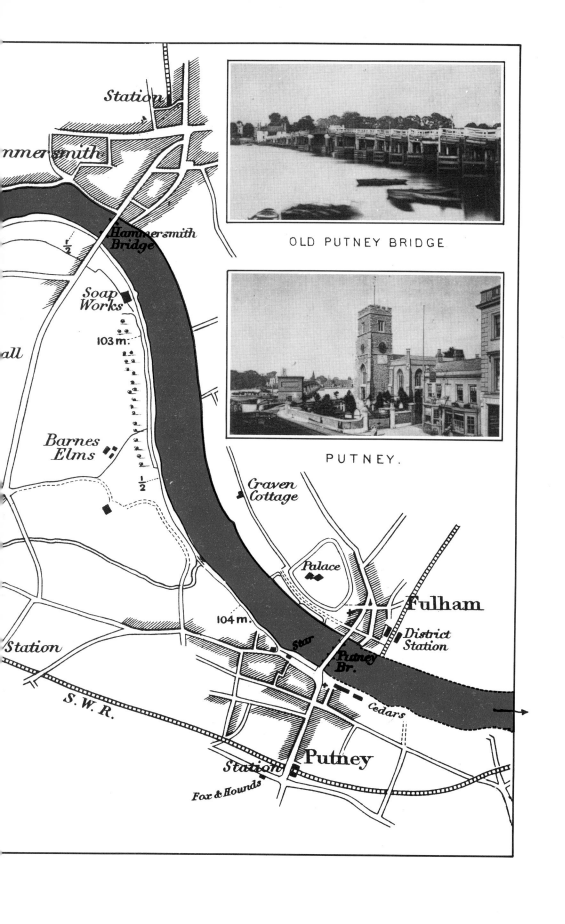

OLD PUTNEY BRIDGE

PUTNEY.

Station

nmersmith

Hammersmith
Bridge

½

Soap
Works

103 m.

all

Barnes
Elms

½

Craven
Cottage

Palace

Fulham

District
Station

Star

Putney
Br.

104 m.

Station

Cedars

S.W.R.

Putney

Station

Fox & Hounds

Strand-on-the-Green tow-path c. 1878

The river is crossed here by a fine lattice girder railway bridge, just below the islands.

Boats Let or Housed – J. Wise, F. Maynard.

Hotels – 'Oxford and Cambridge', 'Star and Garter'.

MORTLAKE

Mortlake Station – SWR, 3 furlongs from the river. Tide flows about 3 hours 30 minutes

From Kew to Mortlake is a dreary bit of the Thames, without any object of interest to break up its loneliness, except on such occasions as the Oxford and Cambridge boat-race, when the river is alive with countless legions of boats of every shape and make, and these increase in numbers when we get near Mortlake, where the racing usually terminates.

The whole length of the broad towing path from Mortlake to Barnes Common on the Oxford and Cambridge day is lined with carriages, two or three deep, and the shore of the river is fairly packed with barges, steam launches, and small pleasure boats, the spectators being numbered by tens of thousands; and Barnes Railway Bridge, from which a grand view of the last part of the race can be well seen, is usually crowded with spectators.

Mortlake owes its notoriety at the present day entirely to its being the end of the match-course beginning at Putney, and is very different on race days from the quiet dull place one finds it in ordinary times. Mortlake was the residence of Dr Dee, the celebrated alchymist in the reign of Elizabeth, who visited him here and treated him with great honour; but although he flourished while she reigned, he afterwards died very poor, and was buried in the churchyard. Mortlake was the site of the first tapestry manufactory in England; it was set up by King James, and extended by Charles, several of the cartoons of Raphael being copied here, as well as other fine designs, but on the fall of the monarchy it was seized and sold as royal property; and the attempt to revive it after the restoration of the king was unsuccessful.

Barnes Railway Bridge is a fine specimen of a girder bridge. Over it the SWR loop line to Kew and Isleworth passes, the station being about half a mile from the river. The river below makes a northern bend, and in this reach a rough south-west wind often throws up a heavy swell when the tide is flowing, making the water unpleasant and at times even dangerous for small boats.

Hotels – The 'Ship', 'Queen's Head' (Mortlake), 'White Hart', 'Bull's Head', Barnes.
Boats Housed and Let – J. Pembery, T. Green.

CHISWICK

Chiswick is next reached, with its well-known ait, the scene of many a hard struggle between contending boats rowing over this course.

Chiswick Church, well known from being the burial place of Hogarth, the painter, is the most prominent object of interest, just above being the Torpedo Launch Works. The house in which Hogarth lived still stands in the lane not far from the church.

Chiswick House, the seat of the Duke of Devonshire, is noted for its beautiful gardens, which would rank still higher were they not eclipsed by the Horticultural Gardens which adjoin them. Both the statesmen Fox and Canning breathed their last within its quiet walls. The ait with its willows partly screens the village from the river; there is a ferry for passengers at the upper end.

HAMMERSMITH

HAMMERSMITH BRIDGE from Barnes Railway Bridge *1 mile 5 furlongs 196 yards; to Putney Bridge, 1 mile 6 furlongs 22 yards. Tide flows about 3 hours 45 minutes*

Hammersmith Stations – Met., SWR, and District, all about 3 furlongs from the bridge.

One of the first noticeable features at Hammersmith is the Mall, with its handsome old elms shading the river. Then follows the new suspension bridge, standing on the same site as the old one, which was a fellow to Marlow Bridge, both being designed by W.T. Clarke. Hammersmith new bridge is in many ways similar to Chelsea, the piers being iron, with the roadway passing through the centre and footways on either side. The foundations are some 30 ft below that of the old bridge down in the London clay, and the structure is in every way stronger than was that of the old bridge. The span is 400 ft in the clear, and the anchors are 40 ft below the ground.

Hammersmith itself is fairly part of London, the High Street boasting omnibuses, trams, and a crush of people, with the usual variety of shops, which prevail in the business outskirts of Town.

A short distance below the bridge stood Brandenburgh House, the residence for a time of Queen Caroline, the unfortunate wife of George IV. She also died here, and soon after the mansion was razed to the ground. Hammersmith Church is some little distance from the river, and scarcely worth the oarsman's visit; but it contains a remarkable monument to Sir Nicholas Crispe, supporting a bronze bust of Charles I. Crispe was enthusiastic for Charles, and devoted himself and fortune to him, sparing no pains by which he could further his royal master's cause, and even on his tomb his heart is placed in a black marble urn 'at his master's feet'.

The river below Hammersmith passes on the right bank Barnes Elms, the residence of Sir Francis Walsingham in the time of Queen Elizabeth; and after him – amongst others – the poet Cowley. A house close by was the residence of Jacob Tonson,* the bookseller, where the Kitcat Club held their meetings, the room being built especially, and hung round with Kneller's famous portraits of the members.

Boats Let or Housed – Biffen and Sons.
Hotels – The 'Rutland', 'City Arms'.

PUTNEY AND FULHAM

PUTNEY BRIDGE from Hammersmith *1 mile 6 furlongs 22 yards; to Wandsworth, about 6 furlongs; to London Bridge, 7 miles 2 furlongs. Tide flows about 4 hours*

Stations – SWR, High Street, about 2 furlongs from the river; (Met. Dist.), Fulham side below the bridge.
Steamboats – Call at Putney Pier every forty minutes during the season.
Putney is the headquarters of many of the Rowing Clubs; and at various

---

* Jacob Tonson, the publisher and bookseller, was secretary for many years of the famous Kit-Cat Club which had been founded in the early part of the eighteenth century. The portraits by Kneller, now in the National Gallery, were painted less than half-length to fit Tonson's dining room and in consequence portraits of this size are termed 'Kit-Cat'.

Thames barges beside the Chelsea Waterworks aqueduct at Putney c. 1878

seasons – particularly that of the annual training and race of the Oxford and Cambridge Eights – is the centre of a fashionable gathering. The London Rowing Club and others have erected new boathouses on the towing-path side, from which a splendid view of the start and racing for the first mile and a half can be obtained.

Putney old bridge was the last of the wooden structures which formerly spanned the Thames. Built upon piles its openings were very small, and although in 1872 an iron girder was thrown across a wider span in the centre, still it was in every way inconvenient, and even dangerous to large craft passing up. It was originally a toll-bridge, but the shareholders were bought out by the Metropolitan Board of Works, the price paid being £58,000, and the bridge declared free. The old bridge was completed in 1729, and removed in 1886, after the opening of the new bridge.

Putney new bridge is a graceful white granite bridge of five segmental arches, and is 44 ft in width between the parapets; the quantity of granite used in its construction was 300,000 cubic feet. It is from the design of Sir Joseph Bazalgette, and the work was carried out by John Waddell and Sons, of Edinburgh and London, the contract being for £240,000. The centre arch has a span of 144 ft; its crown is 20 ft above Trinity high-water mark. The bridge stands a short distance above the old bridge, where the old aqueduct of the Chelsea Water Works used to stand. It was nearly four years in building.

Putney Church stands close to the bridge, and that of Fulham on the other side of the river. Tradition tells us these churches were built by two sisters; but no record remains of the fact. Thomas Cromwell was born at Putney, and also Gibbon, the great historian. Wolsey landed here on his way to Hampton Court, after his dismissal from the Chancellorship.

At Fulham is the residence of the Bishops of London, the palace lying back behind some trees a short distance from the river. A favourite walk near the river's bank, called 'Bishop's Walk', leads from the palace to the church, which latter retains many fine architectural features, and also monuments to several of the bishops, as well as other noted men. The north side of the churchyard is bounded by a picturesque block of almshouses; but beyond these there is nothing to call for notice.

Boats Let or Housed – J.H. Clasper, J.N. Alexander, C. Phelps, G. Cordery, Thompson and Bowes, W. East, J. Robinson.

Hotels – 'Fox and Hounds'; 'Star and Garter', etc.

Fishing – Roach and dace are taken in the reaches above Putney at low tide, if the water is clear, in good numbers.

Fishermen – L. Gibson, C. Gibson, M. Gibson.

Henry Taunt beside Wallingford Bridge c. 1870

LONDON

Few, if any, up-river oarsmen proceed lower than Putney down the river, as the traffic, combined with the tides, takes away all the pleasure which might be derived from the journey. In any case, if proceeding to London by water, take a waterman who knows the river, as the difficulties one way and the other are considerably augmented below Putney.

CAMPING OUT – (IN A BOAT)
By the Editor

'That's just what I should like!' – 'How jolly it must be!' – 'Well, you must enjoy yourself!' – 'I don't wonder at your looking so well!' – 'Ain't you afraid to go to sleep?' These remarks, and fifty others, were passed one evening amongst a circle of friends to whom I had been relating my experiences in camping out. I had just returned from a tour on the Thames, extending over a little more than three months; and I could echo one of the exclamations above by answering, 'It *is* jolly!' I think, too, it will be re-echoed by numbers of persons who have tried it, and thoroughly enjoyed themselves. There are, perhaps a number of reasons why camping out should be enjoyable. First, we live in an age so fast and energetic, that the mind and body get thoroughly used up, demanding in the same interval rest and renewal of vigour, that may fit for after periods of toil; and what greater pleasure can there be to a man, tired out in body and mind, than to throw himself on his back under some wide-spreading tree, and listen to the gentle stream that murmurs by? – or, with rod in hand, to watch the nodding float which, on disappearing, rouses him from a pleasant reverie? And again, the custom of our age is so polite and graceful as to be at times a positive tax upon a man's time and person, making, by contrast, a wild life enjoyable; in fact, the ennui that often takes possession of us would entirely disappear if we were not so highly civilized.

Not that civilization, in its present state, is a failure – far from it; still, it is at times a boon to be able to lay aside the conventionalities of society, and our glimpse of nomadic life forms one of those complementary tones which, in a picture, harmonize and give vigour to the whole composition.

229

THE THAMES OF HENRY TAUNT

It is just the opposite to our usual life; and this is just the reason why camping out is so much liked by those who take it up. They leave behind them those cares of business, those endless accounts, those toils of pleasure that turn night into day; and, in a more simple manner and style, they thoroughly enjoy their food and their rest.

Secondly, camping out is enjoyed because it conduces to more robust health. Excesses of every kind help to wear one out, and this is also one of the causes of lassitude amongst us. When I speak of excesses, I do not mean altogether excesses in eating and drinking, or worse – I mean the ordinary excesses with which a business man meets.

To labour for hours in a foul atmosphere, as many mercantile men in London do, is an excess that damages many of them, and would more, perhaps, were it not for the practice of running out from town to spend the night in a purer atmosphere. To strain every nerve of the brain in getting off orders and merchandise in the shortest space of time possible, and without the omission of the slightest detail; or to be perched at a desk wading through accounts day after day, with scarcely the slightest change of posture – all these are excesses that every City man more or less meets with, and which make the health of the body more delicate. I might go on and complete the catalogue, but the hard-working merchants of our capital will well understand without my going further.

Gentlemen, too, who have no business, still find excesses growing on their time and selves; what more enervating than the midnight party or dance? and how often the 'Pick-me-up', or some other such tonic is required? Camping gives, in exchange for these, more robust health, sounder sleep, and greater enjoyment than anything I know at the same cost.

Ah, there's the *third* reason – cost! There are pleasures that force their majority on some of us in consequence of the deprivation they entail. Camping out does not do this. If properly managed, the cost of the requisite kit is more than saved by the comparatively small expense with which the journey is attended. Perhaps some of the hotel-keepers will not thank me for pursuing this subject; but I am trying to open the river for all, and must tell what I know. I have nothing to say against a single landlord; I know a great many of them, and number some amongst my friends: I am also of the opinion that, instead of injuring them, I shall help to do them good; such is, at least, my wish. Hotels cannot be otherwise than expensive, to a certain extent; they usually have an enormous quantity of out-goings, and in consequence are obliged to recoup themselves; but at the same time I know a great many on the Thames that are thoroughly moderate, and keep down their charges as far as they can. I might go still further, and speak of kindnesses that I know of that have been done – things that would redound to their honour; but it would be unfair to the rest to single out one or two, so I must refrain. However, to our subject. The cost of camping is much less than hotels, as there need be no expenses beyond the necessaries of life, and these are bought first hand. Of course it is an easy thing to make camping out as expensive, or even more so, than living at the hotels. Just go to Fortnum & Mason, or some other purveyors, and order them to send you down a hamper of the greatest delicacies every day, and you will find camping out anything but cheap: you had better go to an hotel. Of course pastry and so on are very nice; they relish now and then first class after the well-cooked fish and steak; but, as a rule, if you camp out much you will rather depend upon what you can do yourself.

There are in the market, at the present time, so many delicacies in a portable form, that one scarcely needs the help of the confectioner otherwise in the camp; and in case such a change is wished for, one can always go to an hotel. I must not waste time further in proving what I think is patent to every one – or why do we have so many picnic parties? – that camping out is thoroughly enjoyable; nay, more, that it is one of the best and cheapest pleasures a man can have; but will call now your attention to another side of the question, the difficulties we meet with. There are two principal modes of camping at present in vogue on the River Thames, and they differ mostly in the sleeping arrangements. The one is to sleep on the shore under a tent, and the other to sleep in the boat, arranged at night for that purpose. The only one advantage that I can see a tent has over the boat is, that a narrower, smaller craft can be used; but there are a number of things to be stated which tell the other way. I must confess I have never tried a tent, but several who have seen my arrangement have left their tents and had their boats arranged for sleeping on my plan, which is very simple, and does not involve any very great expense. My boat is what is termed in Oxford phrase, a Company boat, which is a broad gig with sideseats from the back rail, and an awning (which lets up and down); a locker for food was fitted behind the back rail. The boat is about 22 ft long and 3 ft 9 in wide at the broadest part, and is fitted with the usual mast at the front seat; behind, close to the rudder-post, another short mast is fitted, which serves for a flag-staff during the day. When arranging for night, the awning is raised and fastened, then a side covering of good plain duck secured with strings all round to the iron which holds the awning, and fixed below the seats of the boat with loops, to buttons, thus completely enclosing the middle part of the boat. Between the side seats we place boards fitted on purpose (these go on the side seats, under the cushions, in the day time), and the cushions on the top, with our carpet-bags at the head, form the mattress, which is made complete by a rug thrown over, and blankets or rugs make up the interior of our sleeping-room. On the outside a line is stretched from mast to mast, and on this is threaded the rings of a waterproof, each end ring being stretched to its mast, and eyelet-holes in each corner fastened to buttons on the boat. Thus we have a water-tight, dry sleeping-place, and anything but an uncomfortable one.

Another of its advangtages is that you can sleep where you like. If you choose to cast anchor, you can sleep in the very centre of the stream, where no one can reach you without a boat, or you can sleep up the smallest ditch that you pass on your journey. I found it a very great advantage to have two short iron rye-pecks, with cords attached to the head and stern of the boat; these moored us to any place, and were very convenient at all times. I need hardly say, do not moor on the tow-path bank, or you may chance to find yourself in a mess from the towing-line of some passing barge catching in your upper works.

Camp Furniture – Camp furniture need not be very elaborate. A frying-pan, pot, and kettle, all to fit a fire-holder, will be all that are really required, with the usual plates, mugs, etc., that each one will use; but in every case, if you are camping out, *don't take more than you can help.* You will be surprised how many things you can do without: a wicker-basket will hold your pot, etc., with the necessary fuel for burning, and the other things will go with the food into your locker.

Fuel – Wood is to be bought everywhere in the country, but if a wheelwright or carpenter's shop is handy, try there first. A hatchet will be necessary, to chop it up with.

Matches – Keep your matches dry. We had to go four miles last summer (1872) for some, and to wait two hours for dinner after a hard day's work, through letting them get wet.

Food – 'Nothing like leather' used to be our pass-word when we had beef; and sometimes it was a puzzle, to the one who had not begun, to know whether it was tender or not, as 'nothing like leather' was used to express either. I believe in a good beefsteak, cooked either over the coals or in the pan, when camping out; and this often formed the *piéce de résistance* of our dinner after a stiff day's work. Usually, we had breakfast early (just after our bathe – a thing which helps the appetite very much), and made a good meal; in the middle of the day we feasted on a crust and cheese, and washed it down with a glass of 'home-brew'd', kept for that purpose in a stone bottle; or, failing that, a glass of Thames water, qualified with whisky, or some concentrated milk. When we reached our next camping ground (we usually moved every day), we made our fire and got dinner ready, taking tea with it; and a glass of 'the cratur', with a biscuit, sent us to bed about nine o'clock at night. As I mentioned before, there are a lot of portable things sold in tins, which are uncommonly useful in camping out. The different meats from Australia are included in these, as well as the various potted viands, etc., that are in universal request. Australian meat can be eaten cold just as it is, with a little sauce to flavour it; and if some salad can be got at, a fair dinner or lunch can be made with but little trouble; and then the various ways in which it may be cooked would fill a chapter as long as this, so I must only give you one. Wash and scrape some potatoes and carrots, slice them up, with some onions, and boil till done: then add meat in *quantum suff.*; leave for a few minutes on the fire, flavour, and serve. The Australian meats also make splendid soups, are not much trouble, and, when you cannot get fresh meat, come in very useful, so much so that we always kept them as a reserve. Tea, sugar, butter, and all those sort of things, we kept in tin biscuit-boxes, easily procured at the grocer's. These are always clean, and do not let the things get wet. A ham, too, for 'rashers for breakfast,' is not a bad thing to keep, and the concentrated milk – or that with chocolate – must not be forgotten. Of course, every one must form his own ideas on a subject like this, so I have only indicated those things most essential.

Clothing – An extra suit in a *soft* bag should be taken, in case of wet weather or any other mishap, as well as to be able to change for sleeping at night. Also, of course, the toilet requisites, but not too many of them. The few things I take in that way afford matter for a standing joke with one of my friends; but one doesn't require to spend an hour twice a day preparing for meals and 'parade', when camping out. I spoke of a *soft* bag, as you will require it for a pillow; but if you prefer to use a stiff portmanteau of course you are at liberty to do so; only, don't blame me if your sleep is not so sound as it might be. And that brings me to another point, and one of the most important.

Sleeping – If you don't sleep well, you will not enjoy yourself; and this is why I so much prefer my boat to a tent. We have always a *dry* sleeping apartment. Last summer (1872) was a wet one and I think more rain fell in one week than we had for nine weeks, in the summer before; yet we had no difficulties on account of the rain, as far as sleeping was concerned, but when the wet came on, generally took shelter in bed, or in the daytime moved the middle boards and read, or wrote, or talked, under our awning, as it pleased us most. Only on one occasion did the rain inconvenience us, when the water had risen above the britton-boards, and my man, in hurriedly turning out of bed in the morning, put his foot into it, which he sharply drew back with a shocking

Henry Taunt and his assistants 'camping out in a quiet corner' c. 1870

exclamation. Ugh! In a tent this inconvenience arises: if the ground is at all sloping with water runs down the side of the tent, and underneath you, so that, although you may sleep on water-tight cloth, the damp must get through to a certain extent. I see fellows with camp-bedsteads and so on to keep them from the damp, but I think if their boat were to be used for once as a sleeping place they would leave the tents to take care of themselves.

Ladies have the idea that sleeping on the water is not safe. 'Ar'n't you afraid to go to sleep, in case you should turn over?' is the question generally asked. 'No, never: our boat is a stiff one, and if all three were to roll down on one side (as we have done), it would not even dip.' Ladies don't often camp out, as the limited space renders it inconvenient for them to manage a toilet; but I may tell you I know a lady who has slept in a boat like mine, and thoroughly enjoyed her trip. Some, after camping out all day, go and sleep at an hotel. In the case of delicate persons perhaps this is wise; but it is better to be prepared for sleeping out at all times. It is very pleasant to have a stiff day's pulling, and when fairly tired out, to go to the only inn in the village, and be told there, on inquiring for beds, 'No, sir: we are crammed; haven't a room anywhere!' and find that another, at four or five miles' distance, must be gained if you are bent on trying for accommodation, with the additional uncertainty whether you will get it. This is a case that often happens, and always when you are most tired, or least prepared for it; but if you camp, you just make your hotel wherever you like – the fire is lit, the steak fried, and, with the steaming potatoes straight from the pot, is relished as only a man camping out does relish food. The beefsteaks have a finer flavour, and the potatoes or cabbage (quite fresh, perhaps were growing an hour previously) have a crisper taste than they ever had before.

But I am running away from my subject, or rather, recollections are running away with me, and this won't do; so to sleeping I'll turn again. 'How did you sleep?' is the question generally asked of a guest who has passed the night under your roof; but in camping out one scarcely ever knows even when he does go to sleep, or recollects anything, after rolling himself in his rug, till the morning light peeping through his eyelids rouses and tells him it is time to rise; and then how pleasant the tumble out of bed, and into the fresh, clear stream; a good rub down and an exhilarating run making one ready to eat a good donkey-steak, if nothing more was to be had.

And now a word on cooking and buying things. 'It's no use my camping out, I can't cook,' says one. Don't tell me, but try it; you will soon learn. What not able to cook a beefsteak or chop, boil some potatoes or cabbage, and get up a plain dinner? Well, you are the very person who ought to camp out: it will teach you self-reliance. If you are afraid of the cooking, get your wife or your sweetheart to show you how; don't be ashamed to learn, even from them; you won't find much difficulty about it. And then as to buying. Bread and meat are better had fresh every morning, if possible, as they both get stale very quickly; and the stone jar, which holds enough for the day, filled at the nearest inn (don't take too much, particularly in the daytime, the less the better). Of the other things a stock had better be kept, and replenished, whenever getting short, before they are all gone.

If a party of two or three are together, let each one take his own part – one do the buying, one the cooking, and so on, as division of labour is always an advantage, and each will do his own part best. But I find I have got past the end of my tether, so must end by telling you if you cannot get on do come and take dinner with us; and then you will see for yourself more in five minutes than I can tell you in an hour. I won't promise you an elegant dinner; but if a good plain one will suit your purpose, I shall be very pleased to see you. We don't go in for pastry, but keep rice, which is easily carried; it makes a variety of puddings easily cooked and very palatable. Pancakes, too, are easily managed, and help to remind one of the lady-helps at home, who 'once upon a time' spoilt a whole batch trying to toss them in the orthodox way. We generally have a glass to ask a fellow camper-out to, and something in the shape of grog to set a pipe with in the evening. So, if you will come, you will be made welcome by

Yours very truly,
THE EDITOR

P.S. – As years roll on – and although not yet aged, more than a quarter of a century has passed by since we took our first journey to Cricklade in the Christmas holidays of 1860 – shall we confess that we have become more luxurious, more lazy, or is it that age begins to tell us that we must be extra careful for the future. Perhaps a combination of all these things, with the additional charm of being able, in weather when no other work can possibly be done, to advance the book on 'Old Father Thames' we have been quietly preparing for, all these years, has led us to leave the tented boat for a more permanent covering, as our frontispiece will show. We have had little experience yet in houseboat life, but that little has led us to believe it can be made a thoroughly 'lotus-eating' existence, as under other circumstances it will afford an opportunity of carrying out the contemplated work of half a lifetime. We have removed the locker to the new boat, and shall be pleased to receive the visits of any of our friends who will do us the honour of calling.

May, 1886.

Acknowledgements

The photographs are reproduced by the kind permission of the following:–

Local Studies Library, Oxfordshire County Council Library Service:
pp. 28, 38, 44, 46, 48, 50, 52, 86, 118, 124, 140, 143, 168, 174, 188, 192, 198, 206, 210, 222, 226, 228.

Berkshire Archaeological Society, Reading Museum & Art Gallery:
pp. 26, 60, 64, 72, 76, 80, 82, 84, 92, 94, 100, 104, 108, 110, 114, 126, 128, 130, 144, 150, 152.

Further Reading

Brown, Bryan, *The England of Henry Taunt, Victorian Photographer,* Routledge & Kegan Paul, London, 1973.
Graham, Malcolm, *Henry Taunt of Oxford, A Victorian Photographer,* The Oxford Illustrated Press, 1973.
The Local Studies Library of the Central Library, Oxford has a large holding of published and unpublished material relating to Henry Taunt.

INDEX

Numbers in *Italic* indicate where places appear in the maps